THE
APHORISMS
TO EXPLORE

THE
APHORISMS
TO EXPLORE

SILVESTER DUA–WIAFE

Published in the United Kingdom by
EQUIP PUBLISHING HOUSE

To my beloved wife, Mrs Angelina Dua-Wiafe, whose
unwavering love, patience, and encouragement have been
my constant source of strength. Your partnership in life and
ministry continues to inspire me to press on faithfully.

And to the memory of my dear brother, Elder John Wiafe
(Rtd), whose life, though cut short, remains a testimony
of faith and courage. Your absence is deeply felt, yet your
influence lives on in the lessons you taught, the laughter
you shared, and the legacy you left behind.

This book is for both of you—with love that endures
and gratitude that words can never fully capture.

CONTENTS

ACKNOWLEDGEMENTS

The journey of producing *Aphorisms to Explore* has been shaped by the support, encouragement, and contributions of many people, to whom I owe a great debt of gratitude.

First and foremost, I give thanks to Almighty God, the source of all wisdom and inspiration. Without His guidance and grace, these pages would be empty.

To my family, especially my wife, Mrs. Angelina Dua-Wiafe, and our children, Mrs. Jemima Asamoah, Mrs. Dorcas Doe, Miss Rhoda Serwaa Wiafe, Mr. Enoch Dua-Wiafe, and Mr. James Agyei Dua-Wiafe, thank you for your steadfast love and for always creating space for me to write, reflect, and grow. Your belief in this project gave me the courage to bring it to completion.

To my late brother, Elder John Wiafe (Rtd), whose life continues to remind me of the brevity of time and the urgency of living with purpose, I honour you through these words.

I am deeply grateful to The Church of Pentecost (UK) for being a spiritual home and a nurturing ground. To the ministers, presbyters, officers, and members, your prayers, encouragement, and fellowship have been invaluable. To my local assembly and its leadership, thank you for continually challenging me to grow deeper in faith and service. Many of the lessons and reflections within these pages were inspired by the life and witness of this church family.

I also thank Equip Publishing House for their commitment to excellence in bringing this work to print, and to the editors and reviewers who offered their insight and refinement with care.

Finally, to every reader who takes these words to heart: thank you. May these aphorisms encourage, challenge, and strengthen you on your journey of faith.

INTRODUCTION

Every generation seeks wisdom—truths that endure beyond circumstances, cultures, and time. Yet wisdom is not always found in long discourses or elaborate arguments. Often, it is carried in simple words—concise, memorable, and powerful enough to shape thought and inspire change. This is the essence of an aphorism.

Aphorisms to Explore is a work that brings together timeless expressions of truth, grounded in biblical insight and practical Christian living. It is not merely a compilation of sayings; it is a carefully designed guide for reflection and transformation. Each aphorism is presented not as a slogan to be admired but as a principle to be lived, offering the reader both depth and direction.

This volume is structured to help the reader move from inspiration to application. Many of the aphorisms are illuminated through narratives—simple stories that make abstract truths tangible and relatable. These stories serve as windows, drawing the reader into familiar human experiences while highlighting the presence of God's wisdom within them. Following the stories, concise lists of related aphorisms extend the reflection, and short reflections encourage meditation, personal examination, and prayer.

The beauty of this approach lies in its accessibility. Whether one is a pastor seeking illustrative material, a teacher searching for practical wisdom, or a believer looking for daily encouragement, this book offers something of value. The truths expressed here are not confined to pulpit or classroom; they are equally suited to the home, the workplace, and the private place of prayer.

More importantly, *Aphorisms to Explore* directs the reader consistently towards Christ, the embodiment of divine wisdom. The sayings within remind us that our faith is not a matter of words alone but of lived reality: in our choices, our relationships, our perseverance in trials, and our hope in eternal promises. These aphorisms do not compete with Scripture but flow from it, pointing us back to the Word of God as the ultimate source of light and guidance.

As you turn these pages, you are invited to do more than read. You are invited to engage. Pause over each phrase. Consider its relevance to your own walk of faith. Share it with others. Let these brief sentences and illustrative stories shape your thinking, sharpen your conscience, and stir your spirit. In doing so, you will discover that small words, when rooted in eternal truth, can have immeasurable impact.

It is my prayer that this book will serve as a faithful companion on your journey of discipleship. May it strengthen your resolve to live wisely, encourage you to walk closely with God, and remind you that in Christ, wisdom is not hidden but generously offered to all who seek it.

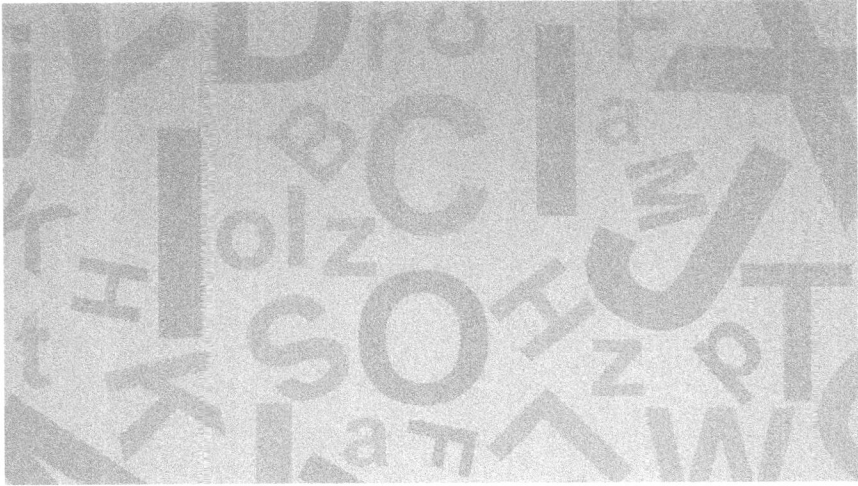

Aphorisms to Explore

APHORISM

A

All Christians work for the same employer

In a small town, three Christians worked in very different roles. Emmanuel was a janitor at the local school, Naomi managed a busy café, and Phillip served as the pastor of the town's only church. Each one diligently performed their tasks, yet each struggled at times with feeling insignificant or unnoticed.

One night, all three had the same dream. In it, they stood before a massive golden throne. A radiant figure—Jesus—smiled at them. He handed each of them a crown and said, "Well done, good and faithful servant."

Emmanuel was stunned. 'But Lord, I only cleaned classrooms.'

Jesus replied, 'Every floor you mopped made the way for children to learn. You worked for Me.'

Naomi spoke next. 'But I only made coffee and sandwiches.' 'And you did it with joy and generosity. You created a space where people found peace. You worked for Me.'

Then Phillip, the pastor, bowed and wept. 'I see now, Lord. We all served the same King.'

In the dream, their earthly jobs faded, and what remained was the love, humility, and diligence they gave—all unto the Lord. When they awoke, each one felt renewed with purpose. The janitor whistled hymns as he worked. The café owner prayed for customers. The pastor thanked God for the unseen ministry of others. They never forgot: they were all employed by Heaven, doing sacred work in different uniforms.

EXPLORE MORE APHORISMS

- A big fall begins with a little stumble.

- A lie may cover your tracks, but it cannot hide the truth.

- A change in behaviour begins with a change in the heart.

- A life lived for Christ is the best inheritance we can leave our children.

- All creation sings God's praise

- A word of encouragement can make the difference between giving up and going on.

- An honest talk with God is the first step in finding peace of mind.

- A person who is not willing to follow is not prepared to lead.

- A good indicator of our spiritual temperature is our eagerness to worship God.

- All work and no play will take the joy of life away.

- As the years add up, God's faithfulness multiplies.

- A sermon is not complete until it's put into practice.

- A mother's heart is the child's classroom.

- A little wisdom is better than a lot of wealth.

- A man is like a lightbulb; flip the switch and he is immediately turned on. A woman is more like an iron; flip the switch and she takes time to warm up.

- A man is affected by what he sees and a woman by what she hears and feels.

- Are you moving your tent near Sodom?

- A passing bird on the tree, so is mankind.

- As you renew your mind with scripture daily, your faith will grow, your outlook will be altered, and every area of your life will start to change for the better.

- At your job, in your home, in your personal life, in your church, faithfulness is what God seeks in every situation.

- A study diet of sound doctrines is necessary for believers to grow strong in their faith.

- A guilty conscience is a warning signal God placed inside us that goes off when one has done wrong.

- A rough start does not mean a rough end.

- A life devoted to things is a dead life, a stump; a God-shaped life is a flourishing tree.

- At the appointed time, you will laugh.

- A house is not a Home.

- Acknowledging your powerlessness is the first step to victory.

- Acknowledging your powerlessness is not the same as giving in to defeat

- Are you struggling with injustice when it seems others are getting away with wrongdoing?

- Agreeing with what you understand is agreement. Agreeing with what you don't understand is not agreement but faith.

- All life is only a temporary arrangement.

- A tree is not known by association but by its fruits.

- As caterpillars turn into butterflies, so does time; it will change.

- As we imitate Christ and our children imitate us, they will have godly models to follow.

- A child who is taught to obey will be a child who learns self-control and true wisdom.

- A bad wife or husband is preferable to a bad in-law.

- A funnel has a wide and a narrow end. Some people enter life at the narrow end and come out at the wide end. Others enter at the wide end and come out at the narrow end. That is how people are different and progress through life in various ways.

- A call for Christians to show love is the face of hatred, patience in response to trouble and peace in moments of conflict.

- All creation finds both its origin and fulfilment in Christ Jesus.

- An old song tells us to count our blessings, but it is not possible; they are too many.

- A woman complained to her pastor that she had noticed a lot of repetition in his sermons. "Why do you do that?" The pastor replied, "People forget."

- An old man said, "There is only so much I can fit in my brain. I have to delete something before I can remember something new."

- A little faith is faith, as a spark of fire is fire.

- A leader is a Servant.

- All that God created on the sixth day was good except when it was not good because man was alone. (Gen 2:18)

- As you become wiser, you will talk less and listen more.

- A wise man is someone who thinks twice before saying nothing.

- Anytime I want to become like you, I can. But I can never become the person I was before I made that decision (a word to the wise).

- After a spiritual mountain top experience, you must take what you have received and share it with those in the valley.

- At times, it can be tempting to give to God our leftovers.

- At the final sacrifice for the sins of the world was being made, God closed the door to all human eyes and turned out the lights of heaven. For three hours, the eternal transaction for your sin and mine was between the Father and the Son alone.

- A year is said to be 31,557,600 seconds, and our God takes good care of every second in our lives.

- As a Christian, don't live a life on the surface of the spiritual ocean.

- All spiritual gifts are equally important.

- As far as the spiritual gifts are concerned, it does not matter who gets the credit as long as the job gets done and God gets the glory.

- An encyclopaedia filled with knowledge has no value if it is never used.

- As you mind your earthly duties, keep heaven in mind.

- Adversities are often blessings in disguise.

- Adam and Eve were given only one commandment to obey but they failed (Accident and Emergency – A&E).

- A healthy heart beats with love for Jesus.

- A woman's heart is an ocean of secrets.

- A child will not die just because his mother's milk is dry.

- A bird does not damage its feathers because of bad weather.

- A contented customer will not only recommend an organisation to others but may also buy other products that the other organisation offers.

- Adam loves Eve and Eve loves Adam and they have sweet fellowship with each other. This is God's plan for a family unit.

- A bad decision can delay you from reaching your destiny.

- Avoid double standards as a child of God.

- A Christian should desire to move towards Jesus, and not away from him.

- Always keep a cool head and a warm heart.

REFLECTION

These aphorisms invite us to reflect deeply on our Christian walk. They convey principles or insights that, when lived out, can shape our faith and actions. Consider how these truths apply to your current season of life and how God might be using them to draw you closer to Him.

APHORISM

B

Be the Strongest Link, Not the Weakest Link

During a military training camp, a group of recruits were assigned a task: carry a large wooden log across a muddy field. The task required every recruit to hold their share of the weight. At first, everyone struggled in unison, but soon one recruit, Adom, began to slack. Tired, he shifted more and more of the burden to the others.

As the weight increased, tempers flared. 'Adom, we need you.' shouted another recruit. Embarrassed and convicted, Adom took a deep breath. He repositioned his hands, squared his shoulders, and began lifting more than before.

As Adom dug deep and found strength, others around him were inspired. The team finished the task quicker than expected.

Later that night, the drill sergeant gathered them around. 'Every mission you face in life, in faith, in family—someone is watching. You can be the weakest link that causes a collapse, or the strongest that carries others through. Today, Adom became the strongest link.'

The words stayed with Adom long after training ended. When he became a youth pastor years later, he often reminded young people:

'Don't complain about the weight. Be the one who lifts. Strength isn't always about muscles—it's about heart.'

EXPLORE MORE APHORISMS

- Build people up, don't tear them down.

- Because we all need forgiveness, we should all be quick to forgive.

- Because Christ lives, death is not a tragedy but triumph.

- Be a man who lived better than he preached.

- Before we can pray, "Lord, thy Kingdom come," we must be willing to pray, "my Kingdom go."

- Be alert for the opportunities God gives you and take full advantage of them.

- Better is the end than the beginning.

- Beliefs are only as strong as the actions they produce.

- Be around people who are going where you are trying to go.

- Burnt out begins with weariness.

- Before you take on the future, recall God's goodness to you in the past.

- Blessed is the man who knows his petrol is empty.

- Because of God's promise, we have hope beyond physical death.

- A born-again Christian is given certain gifts, and Christ expects you to use them.

- Borrow the idea, don't borrow the money.

- Because you are connected to him, a thousand will fall on your left hand and ten thousand on your right hand.

- Businesses are not run by degrees.

- Be careful what you do because little eyes are watching you.

- The Bible is a book we can trust and a story we can believe.

- By spiritual tools we refer to Bible study, prayer, service, worship, generosity, friendship, and more, are crucial tools to awareness of God's blessings.

- Bad money always looks good.

- Believe nothing and be on your guard against everything.

- Better to be pruned to grow than cut to burn.

REFLECTION

The statements remind us of a foundational Christian truth. They call us to examine how we live, how we influence others, and how we reflect Christ's nature in practical ways. Whether they point us toward resilience, encouragement, forgiveness, or humility, these aphorisms are important prompts to align our lives more fully with the gospel.

APHORISM
C

*Children's ears may be closed
to advice, but their eyes
are open to examples*

Little Adeapena was six years old and full of questions. She often sat quietly in the living room watching her father, Kwame, who was a deacon in the local church. Every morning, Kwame would sit by the window with his Bible, reading and whispering prayers. He never forced Adeapena to join, nor did he preach at her. He just lived his faith.

Years went by. In her teens, Adeapena rebelled. She stopped going to church, rolled her eyes at devotionals, and claimed religion was outdated. But every morning, her father still prayed.

One rainy night, Adeapena came home heartbroken. A friend had betrayed her. As she passed by the living room, she paused—Kwame was praying, as usual.

Tears in her eyes, she asked, 'Daddy, can you pray for me too?'

Kwame simply nodded, held her hands, and prayed with love and assurance. That night, something changed. Not because of a sermon, but because of years of a silent, faithful example.

Years later, Adeapena, now a teacher, was asked what brought her back to faith. She smiled and said:

'I never listened to my dad's words when I was young. But I watched his life. And his life preached louder than any sermon ever could.'

EXPLORE MORE APHORISMS

- Christians stand strong when they stand together.

- Christ's love creates unity in the midst of adversity.

- Christians who bury their gifts make a grave mistake.

- Children of the King have no reason to live like paupers.

- Christ's empty tomb guarantees our full salvation.

- Contentment is not getting what we want but being satisfied with what we have.

- Compromise represents a far greater risk than courage.

- Christ will do the miraculous, but He often chooses to involve us.

- Can you take the first step in restoring peace whenever it has been lost?

- Christ breaks down every barrier that threatens relationships.

- Clinging to a relationship whose season has ended will only lead to heartbreak.

- Choices are powerful, be careful when choosing.

- Change brings challenges.

- Cultures sometimes clash.

- Choose the right path, follow it and it will end well.

- Concerns for our needs to be met can send us searching in many directions.

- Christ is the answer.

- Check me out, it is the Lord's doing.

- Countless hours, persistent effort and constant improvement make the difference between ambition and success.

- Confession brings honesty and spiritual growth.

- Christians are to be difference makers in the world.

- Conditionally, we are a work-in-progress and Jesus would not give up on us.

- Choosing the wrong occupation will put you in the wrong place, with the wrong people.

- Coaches show athletes they have potential by investing in their development.

- Compare and contrast Positioned Blessing in Christ and Practical Blessings of the righteous living.

- Control the controllable and leave the uncontrollable to God.

- Christians are like coals of fire – together they glow, apart they grow cold.

- Celebrating the Lord's supper should move our hearts to mend our ways.

- Calvary reveals the vileness of our sin and the vastness of God's love.

- Christ paid a debt He did not owe to satisfy a debt we owe.

- Christ's soldiers fight best on their knees.

- Creation is filled with signs that point to the creator.

- Changing your thoughts is the key to a new beginning.

- Christ Jesus will return you to your Garden of Eden someday, sometime, so rest assured.

- Church service is not a long service award.

- Coming together is a beginning; Keeping together is progress; working together is success.

REFLECTION

The aphorisms offer clear and thought-provoking messages for our spiritual journey. They urge us to embody our beliefs in visible ways, whether through unity, service, or faithful witness. As you meditate on these truths, consider how they challenge your current mindset or actions, and how they might inspire you to grow more like Christ.

APHORISM

D

Don't plan to repent at the 11th hour – you may die at 10:59hrs

Manu was the kind of man everyone admired. Sharp in mind, charming in speech, and always dressed like success itself. He had just turned thirty and was already managing a team of twenty in one of Accra's leading tech firms. But while his achievements grew, his heart remained closed to God.

His grandmother, Nana Yaa, prayed for him daily. Every time he visited her, she would say, 'My son, remember your Creator in the days of your youth.' Manu would kiss her forehead and respond with a grin, 'Grandma, I'll get to that. You know I'll repent at the right time—the 11th hour.'

One Sunday, he attended church for her sake. The preacher's voice echoed: 'Today, if you hear His voice, do not harden your heart.' Manu sat quietly, feeling something stir inside. But the moment passed. He stepped outside, took a call, and returned to his world of deals and deadlines.

Then came the afternoon no one expected. While he was driving on the motorway on his way to sign a major contract that would secure his promotion, music blasting, heart racing with ambition, he barely noticed the truck until it was too late.

Witnesses said the impact was deafening. Emergency services arrived swiftly, and Manu was rushed to the hospital with a severe head trauma and internal bleeding.

At the hospital, Nana Yaa arrived, Bible in hand, her lips quivering. She held his unresponsive hand and whispered, 'Jesus is near, Manu. Call on Him.' But he never stirred. Machines beeped. Minutes ticked by. At 10:59 PM, the flatline came. Manu was gone.

His funeral was packed. Friends, colleagues, even clients came. Some cried from guilt; others from fear. The pastor, with tears in his eyes, said, 'Manu knew the truth. He planned to come to God. But he never planned to die so soon.'

That day, dozens responded to the altar call. Among them was Manu's younger cousin, Yaw, who said, 'I won't gamble with my soul. I choose Christ today.'

Manu's life was bright, but his delay was costly. His story now lives as a warning: Salvation is not a future event—it's a present invitation. Don't plan for the 11th hour. You may die at 10:59.

EXPLORE MORE APHORISMS

- Don't wait till the last minute to repent; any moment may be your last.

- Death is the last chapter of time, but the first chapter of eternity.

- Devotion to Jesus is the key to spiritual passion.

- Delay is not denial, so keep on praying.

- Do you want to be like Jesus? Replace curiosity with compassion.

- Don't believe everything you hear.

- Don't pass it on, pass it back to where it came from.

- Duty is ours, events are God's (Matt. Henry's comment on Exodus 2)

- Doing nothing has critics; doing something also has critics.

- Don't throw the baby out with the bath water.

- Don't make major decisions during a storm.

- Displaying favouritism can be crippling in a family.

- Difficulty turns a platform upon which the Lord displays His power.

- Do yourself a favour, don't blame the devil.

- Do you have a reservation in heaven?

- Don't be intimidated by the world but be motivated by the word.

- Delivered but damaged? Look to Jesus.

- Don't despise the days of small beginnings.

- Decisions are taken with the head and not the heart.

- Discover your God-given talents, develop them to the fullest and use them to glorify Him and bless others.

- Don't die with your music still inside you.

- Declaration of independence, a sales contract, a legal marriage certification provide a record of the past, assurance in the present and hope for the future.

- Don't let someone else's limited thinking limit you.

- Don't go to the wrong address, for Jesus' address has changed.

- Does God want me to succeed? Yes, but He won't drop success into your lap. He promised to "bless all the work of your hands" (Deut. 28:12).

- Don't just think about the problem, think about the Lord.

- Do you have a problem in your marriage? Don't give up, try a new attitude.

- Do you have a problem in your business? Don't throw in the towel; look for a new approach, reorganise and re-focus on your goal.

- Don't surrender to discouragement. Don't give an inch. Fight every step of the way.

- Discover God's plan for your life and live by it.

- Don't end up regretting time and opportunities you wasted.

- Doing right is never wrong.

- Don't be discouraged if things seem slow. The Holy Spirit works on His own schedule.

- Don't let anxiety replace your faith.

- Don't worry today, remember, with God leading us, we can make it through the wilderness.

- Don't allow the devil to use selective memory to deceive you into doubting God.

- Do you read the Bible to find out what it says or just read it to prepare a sermon?

- Do not confuse a ring for love.

- Don't say my Bible is silent when you don't open it the whole week.

- Do you have a day of rest, or are you at work 365 days, 7 days a week (24/7)? Have a day of rest, please, even God had a rest day.

- Don't compromise, cover up and cut corners to get what you want.

- Don't neglect your conscience, it is either a healthy conscience or an unhealthy conscience.

- Don't let the fear of what might happen cause you to miss an opportunity.

- Devotion is evidenced by action not words.

- During those three hours of darkness while Jesus was on the cross, God the Father and His Son did business alone.

- Don't allow yourself to catch the frustration of depression.

REFLECTION

The wisdom in these aphorisms speaks directly to the urgency and practicality of living out our faith. They compel us to act with intention, to trust God's timing, and to honour our responsibilities in the light of eternity. Take a moment to evaluate how these truths resonate with your walk with God and what changes they might prompt in your priorities.

APHORISM

E

---

*Every child of God should
have a growing likeness
to the Father*

At ten years old, Samuel was already nicknamed 'Little Pastor.'
Not because he preached, but because he mimicked his father,
Reverend Nketiah. He followed him to early morning prayers,
sat quietly beside him during counselling sessions, and even
stood next to him at the church door to greet members.

One Sunday, while walking home, a neighbour saw Samuel
help an elderly woman carry her basket across a muddy path.
She smiled and said, 'You're just like your father.'

Years passed. Samuel faced temptations that tugged at his
integrity. At university, he was invited into circles that mocked
holiness and valued rebellion. He struggled silently. One night,
after a party that left him feeling empty, he found himself
staring into the mirror.

He whispered, 'Is this what being a child of God looks like?'

That night, he opened his Bible—one that had gathered dust. The verse he landed on shook him: *"Be imitators of God, as dearly loved children."* (Ephesians 5:1)

Conviction broke him. Tears flowed. He knelt beside his bed and said, 'Father, I want to reflect You again.'

From that moment, things changed. His friends noticed a shift—not in his speech alone, but in his peace, kindness, and unwavering choices. His roommates once teased, 'You're becoming a pastor like your dad.' Samuel only smiled. He was more than his father's son—he was God's.

Years later, now a mentor to many, Samuel would often say:

'It's not enough to bear the title "child of God." We must bear His likeness. Love like Him. Walk like Him. Forgive like Him. That's when the world truly sees the Father.'

EXPLORE MORE APHORISMS

- Every loss leaves a space that only God's presence can fill.

- Each life is like a book, lived one chapter at a time.

- Every Christian is a steward of the gifts and grace of God.

- Even if you are pushed to the back of the crowd, you can be assured that, even there, Jesus will find you.

- Every setback is already arranged to come back.

- Every relationship in your life is for a reason and a season.

- Everyone can be a leader. It is about influence, not titles.

- Every woman of beauty without grit is guilty.

- Eve went window shopping and brought a bill Adam could not pay.

- Every Christian goes through occasional "dark night" on their journey of faith.

- Each day of our lives, we make a deposit in the memory banks of our children.

- Enthusiasm will take you where talent alone cannot.

- Everyone needs a word of encouragement, an act of kindness, and the gift of friendship.

- Even fools are thought wise if they keep silent (Prov. 17:28).

- Every time you say "yes" to something, you are saying "no" to other options.

- Every other religion is about what you do, do, do but Christianity is about what has been done, done, done by Christ.

- Every other religion is about human beings trying to get to God, but Christianity is God coming down and reaching human beings.

- Esther found herself in a mess; there was a nation-saving message in the mess.

- Every Christian is a minister and has a ministry.

- Experience is only profitable if we learn from it.

- Everything belongs to God.

- Every saint has the past and sinner has a future.

- Engagement that lasts long does not upgrade to a wedding.

REFLECTION

The insights in the aphorisms encourage a deeper awareness of God's presence and purpose in our lives. Each phrase points us toward a more grounded and hopeful walk of faith, reminding us of our identity in Christ, our stewardship of His gifts, and the assurance of His companionship through every season. Reflect on how these truths shape your perspective today.

APHORISM

F

For a good night's rest, rest in the Lord

Priscilla was exhausted—physically, emotionally, and spiritually. Her startup business had hit financial turbulence, her marriage felt distant, and her prayer life was hanging by a thread. Every night, she lay in bed tossing and turning, her mind racing with what-ifs and worst-case scenarios.

One evening, after crying silently beneath her covers, she reached for her Bible. It opened to Psalm 4:8: *"In peace I will lie down and sleep, for you alone, Lord, make me dwell in safety."* She sat up, startled by how the verse met her moment.

That night, she made a decision. She would surrender—not just her burdens but her anxious grip on control. She turned off her phone, knelt by her bed, and whispered: 'Lord, I can't hold this anymore. You take it. I choose to rest—in You.'

The sleep that followed wasn't shallow or restless. It was deep and healing. She awoke not to a fixed situation, but to a settled spirit. From that night on, Priscilla developed a new habit. Before bed, she would read Scripture, journal her thoughts, and pray short, honest prayers. Her sleep improved. So did her clarity.

When asked how she managed peace amid chaos, she smiled and said:

'Rest isn't the absence of problems—it's the presence of God in the midst of them. For a good night's rest, I don't count sheep anymore. I speak with the Shepherd.'

EXPLORE MORE APHORISMS

- Fellowship builds up and binds us together.

- Fire refines God, adversity refines man.

- Follow Christ, not the crowd.

- Freedom is not the right to do as you please; it is the liberty to do as you ought.

- 'Foxhole Christianity' turn to God only when they get into a jam.

- Forward focuses on areas of life that if biblically addressed can propel you into the future.

- Fight a gloomy outlook. Attitude is a little thing, but it makes a big difference.

- From time to time, you will experience fatigue, frustration, failure and fear. Standing on God's promises and drawing on His strength, you can choose not to get discouraged.

- Faith is not about perfection but direction.

- Faith in God's goodness keeps hope alive.

- Faith and trust are the antidotes for fear and anxiety.

- Feeling curious about somebody's problem? Shift into Jesus' mode and move past the point of curiosity to his or her point of need.

REFLECTION

These beautiful phrases are brief but powerful reminders of deeper biblical truths. They invite us to think about trust, resilience, relationships, or purpose in the light of our faith. As you ponder these aphorisms, ask yourself how God may be calling you to live this truth more fully in your daily walk.

APHORISM
G

*God can mend your broken
heart, but you must give
Him all the pieces*

Akosua had loved deeply and lost tragically. Her fiancé, Joe Sam, had been her anchor during university—her encourager, her best friend, her future. When he passed away in a sudden accident just weeks before their wedding, her world shattered.

She stopped attending church. Worship songs made her cry. She still believed in God, but her heart was fragmented, and she didn't know how to pray anymore. 'If You're really good, Lord, why didn't You stop it?' she often whispered through tears.

Months later, during a quiet moment, her aunt gave her a handwritten note. It read:

"God can mend your broken heart, but you must give Him all the pieces."

The words struck her. She had been holding on to certain memories, questions, and pain like shards of glass—afraid to let go, afraid to bleed again.

That night, Akosua laid everything bare before God: her anger, sorrow, disappointment, even the joy she feared she'd never feel again. It was messy, tearful, and honest. But it was surrender.

In the months that followed, healing came—slowly, gently. Not by forgetting Joe Sam, but by remembering him through grace, not grief. She began writing again. She rejoined her church's grief support group. One day, she shared her story with a young widow who said, 'If God healed you, maybe He can heal me too.'

Years later, Akosua would often tell others:

'God is the best heart surgeon I know. He never wastes our pain, but He can only work with what we place in His hands.'

EXPLORE MORE APHORISMS

- God often uses bitter experiences to make us better.

- God speaks to those who take time to listen.

- God blesses us so that we can be a blessing to others.

- God gives blessings to us so we can give glory to Him.

- God doesn't have a Plan B. His plan is you. You are the answer (Said by Gary Haugen)

- God places us in unique circumstances where our abilities match the problem He wants to fix.

- God's call may come at any time, so be ready all the time.

- God never puts you in the wrong place to serve Him.

- God's syllabus for His children's education includes training through hardship.

- God is looking for ordinary people to do extraordinary work.

- God's plans always lead to victory.

- Give God what is right, not what is left.

- God giving deserves our thanking.

- Good health and good sex go together.

- God takes our "enough" and makes it more than enough.

- Good planning and hard work lead to prosperity (Prov 21.5 NLT).

- God will do it through you, as long as you remember you can't do it without Him.

- God makes sure everything that needs to happen, happens at the right time.

- God moves at the appropriate speed to make sure you arrive safely at the destination He has planned for you.

- God's work is usually done behind the scenes in the ordinary things of life.

- God, I don't understand it, but I trust You, should be your prayer.

- God would put a difference between those who mislead and those who are misled.

- God will surely give you a prophet.

- God answers to His word, not to emotions.

- God lovingly restores those who turn back to Him.

- God took something shameful and weak (death on the cross) and made it the foundation of wisdom and power.

- God does the imaginable.

- God reshapes our hearts and desires, transforming us from the inside out.

- Give your attention to the things of God and it will determine where you end.

- God, in his appointed time, will fill your mouth with laughter and you will laugh, ha ha!

- God is into rewards; make sure you get one.

- God will gather all our shame and failures and wash them away with his wide-sweeping grace.

- God's mercy heals and redeems the most painful places in our souls – even the ones we have hidden for so very long.

- God's mercy sweeps away all our guilt, washes away every regret and sets us on high.

- God's eternal plan and His blessing will arrive in time.

- God will make your child wise beyond his age.

- Get Jesus in your boat and the storm will cease.

- God's correction is not rejection; it is proof of His love.

- God's purpose in discipline is to develop you to your highest potential.

- God knows us, He has a roadmap for our lives.

- God made us for Himself and our hearts are restless til they rest in Him.

- God's Holiness is best seen in His hatred of sin.

- God brings a situation to bring revelation.

- God will not give more than your capacity.

- God's grace is amazing.

- God did for Cain what Cain should have done for Abel.

- God will work it for good, the problem you are going through.

- God's strength works best in weakness.

- Give your children a listening ear and reward them graciously with love.

- God also reveals Himself in these four ways:

  » Through the Seen Word

  » Through the Spoken Word

  » Through the Written Word

  » Through the Incarnate Word

- Godly motivations move us to dream big, but unwise motivations inspire us to retreat.

- God's word is settled in heaven (Ps 119:89).

- God's promises in writing is the Bible.

- God does not call the qualified but qualifies the unqualified.

- God's word says our labour in the Lord is not in vain. Take this assurance like a broom to sweep every discouragement out of your heart.

- Good looks are deceptive.

- Give yourself time to incorporate wisdom into your words, avoiding those that make you feel intimidated or inferior.

- God is always working in the background for more and much better than you know or understand.

- God has your name in His book.

- God's words are worth much and cost little.

- God's grace covers all the mistakes and wrong decisions we could ever make.

- God turned "not good" into "good" when Eve was created from the rib of Adam (Genesis 2:18).

- God is always at work and He always sees the end from the beginning.

- Great customer service begins with being employee-focused and customer-focused second.

- God's grace is the only thing that can dissolve sin completely.

- God can hear unspoken prayers and answer them.

- Get out of the critic's seat of your children and become their greatest supporter.

- Gift of love (John 3:16).

- God's love is unsearchable and His grace is amazing

- God gave us two ears and one mouth because we need to listen twice as much as we talk – quick to listen and slow to speak.

- Good listeners are not born, they are bred.

- Good listening is hearing what they think, mean, feel, not what you imagine they do.

- Good listeners don't rush to a conclusion even if what they say does not quite add up; keep listening.

- God will use people to bless you, but He alone is your source of provision.

- God is the source and strength of your progress.

- God's law pinpoints our problem; God's grace provides the solution.

- God is everywhere, he's available every time and listens always.

- Grace and Mercy are unearned blessings.

- God is a being who is both eternal and uncreated.

- God is not interested in religion; He is interested in relationships.

- 'Good Friday' is good because He (Jesus) brought God's forgiveness for sins.

- God rested on the seventh day to reflect on all He had made, and behold, it was very good. God wants us to have, similarly, a day of rest to think about Him and all His wonderful creation and salvation.

- God's blessings are not just here today and gone tomorrow.

- God's love in our hearts gives us a heart for the lost.

- God knows what you don't know.

- God delights in turning crucifixions into resurrections.

- Go fast alone or go far together.

- God, not people, holds the key to your future (Jesus yesterday, today and tomorrow).

REFLECTION

The truth behind the aphorisms offers both comfort and challenges. They remind us of God's sovereignty, His grace, and His involvement in our everyday lives. Let these reflections deepen your trust in His plan and renew your commitment to honouring Him with all He has given you.

APHORISM
H

---

*Happiness depends on
happenings, but joy
depends on Jesus*

Eric had everything going for him—at least on the outside.
A good job, a new car, and a social media feed full of smiling
photos. But deep down, his joy was fragile. Whenever things
didn't go his way—when a deal fell through or someone
disappointed him—his emotions would spiral.

One Sunday, dragged to church by a friend, he heard a message
about joy. The pastor said, 'Happiness is like the weather—it
changes daily. But joy is like the sun—it's always there, even
behind the clouds.' Those words stuck with Eric.

That same week, Eric's car broke down and his promotion
was given to someone else. As frustration bubbled inside, he
found himself recalling the sermon. He opened his Bible and
read John 15:11: *"'These things I have spoken to you, that My
joy may be in you, and that your joy may be full.'"*

'Lord,' he prayed quietly, 'if Your joy is different from mine,
I want it. Teach me.'

That prayer marked a turning point. He started seeking Christ—not just His blessings, but His presence. Over time, Eric found stability. Even when life didn't feel perfect, a strange peace carried him. He began serving at church, mentoring others who, like him, were chasing happiness but missing joy.

Now, when asked why he still smiles during tough times, Eric says:

'Joy isn't about what's happening around me—it's about Who is living inside me. Happenings change. Jesus doesn't.'

EXPLORE MORE APHORISMS

- Honesty pays great dividends and that is God's approval and clear conscience.

- Happiness is not a destination but a day-by-day journey.

- How easy it is to know what is right and yet not do it.

- Heavy upon one becomes light upon many.

- His destiny was the cross, His purpose was love and His reason was you.

- Heaven is a realm of unsurpassed joy, unfading glory, undiminished bliss, unlimited delights and unending pleasures.

- Habits create character and character determines destination.

- Husbands, beware of buying wrong ideas from your wife – Sarah sold one to Abraham and it became a family problem.

- Heaven is not a reward for doing good.

- Happiness is discovered when we sympathise with those around us who suffer.

- Hardship is often the process by which God purifies the gold of our faith. He drank a cup of wrath without mercy, that we might drink a cup of mercy without wrath.

- He left his case in the hands of God who always judges fairly.

- Hold fast to God, drawing strength and encouragement from the wise.

- Hear and listen to the wise words of your mother.

- He took over sin so we could take His righteousness.

- Harbouring bitterness will not change the other person, but it will change you and not for better, but worse.

- Humility can be sought but never celebrated.

REFLECTION

These mind-provoking aphorisms touch on the deeper realities of Christian living. They help to distinguish between fleeting feelings and enduring truths, between worldly values and eternal principles. Let them guide you in evaluating where your peace, purpose, and priorities truly lie in Christ.

APHORISM

I

If sins were not deceitful,
they would not seem delightful

Kwame was the class clown, the charmer, and the risk-taker. He loved the rush of breaking rules, the thrill of rebellion, and the applause that often followed. At first, it all seemed harmless—skipping church, lying to cover weekend escapades, and mocking anything that seemed 'too holy.'

His grandmother, Nana Adwoa, would caution him gently: 'Sin will always look sweet until it shows you its teeth.' But Kwame laughed it off. After all, everyone else was doing it.

Then came the night when everything changed. Caught in a scandal that cost him his scholarship and stained his reputation, Kwame sat in the university chapel alone. No crowd. No laughter. Just silence and consequences.

He looked up at the simple wooden cross on the wall and whispered, 'Why didn't I see this coming?' A quiet voice within him replied, 'Because sin doesn't show you the end—it only sells you the thrill.'

That night, Kwame wept for the first time in years—not because he got caught, but because he finally saw the trap. He returned home, confessed to his family, and began the long road of rebuilding. It was difficult, but not without hope.

Years later, speaking to a group of teenagers, Kwame held nothing back. 'If sins were ugly from the start, we'd run from them. But they come dressed as fun, freedom, or fame. Don't be fooled. What delights for a moment can destroy for a lifetime. But thank God, grace is greater still.'

EXPLORE MORE APHORISMS

- In the drama of life, God is the Director behind the scenes.

- If you panic and run, you might miss the miracle.

- It is better to bite your tongue than to let it bite someone else.

- It is not how long you live that counts, but how you live.

- In every desert of trial, God has an oasis of comfort.

- In the race of life, it takes discipline to finish strong.

- In a world that "could not care less", Christ wants us to care more.

- If our body, soul and spirit are to function at their best, time is needed for renewal (for leisure and rest).

- If you use time well in marriage, you are on your way to getting many other things right.

- It is never wrong to do right. It is never right to do wrong and it is always right to do right.

- If you don't allow yourself time for physical rejuvenation and spiritual restoration, you will burn out.

- If your heart is heavy today, you are trying to carry too much.

- It is:

  » God the Father, to whom we have our access.

  » God the Son through whom we have our access and God the Holy Spirit, by whom we have our access.

- In a moment of crisis, judgement, terror and need, the world turns to those who know their God.

- If you consult God, "He will show you which path to take (Prov. 3:6 NLT).

- If God is the foundation of your strategy, it will work best.

- Ignorance of the scriptures is ignorance of Christ.

- It costs to follow Jesus Christ, but it costs more not to.

- In Jesus Christ, former enemies unite in love.

- If you want to know what God is like, look at Jesus.

- If God has a plan for you, He will fetch you from the background and bring you into the foreground.

- If the love of God within you wears a servant's towel, you will serve others.

- If possible, put significant decisions on hold until your storm passes.

- Iron sharpens iron (Prov. 27:17).

- If you are not thinking correctly, you are not living correctly.

- Integrity is not attempting to do damage control, but is who you are when nobody is looking.

- It is hard to stay on purpose if you don't know what your purpose is.

- It is always easier to pull someone down than it is to lift them up.

- If you want to soar with eagles, you cannot run around with turkeys.

- It is important to choose your friends wisely.

- If you don't know the will of God in your plan, you frown at God.

- It sounds 'foolish' to say that salvation could come through a cross, a death marked by weakness, defeat and humiliation.

- Imagine a home with no negative experience, that is heaven and that is our home.

- It is not about the dress but the wearer of the dress.

- In the walk of faith, sometimes you come to a sign that says "expect delays".

- Impatience is spiritual immaturity; learn to be patient.

- If the handshake goes beyond the elbow, it is no longer a handshake but a grab.

- In the eyes of God, you are loved, beautiful and gifted, so don't put yourself down.

- In our pain, we might beg God to quickly end the process; He knows best.

- It takes one to know one.

- In Christ, the old labels are no longer useful.

- I encourage you to tap into the true source of life (Jesus Christ), for there is no other place to live and thrive than being attached to him.

- If you need to cut some things out of your life that are distracting you from your commitment to Christ, today is the day; don't delay.

- If you are not abiding in the Vine, then you have no hope and promise.

- It is not about what you are running to but what you are running from that counts.

- It is not about you and your gifts; it is about the giver of the gifts.

- If you never take a risk, you will never overcome.

- If God has called you for a purpose, know this: Nothing will prosper against you and God's purpose for your life.

- If we see only the problems, we will be defeated, but if we see the possibilities in the problems, we can have victory.

- If you are facing some hard decisions today, claim Psalm 32:8 – He will guide you with His eye.

- Information means you know something and knowledge means you know what to do.

- It was not Jesus' bill to pay but out of grace, He did pay for it for you, so be thankful.

- If you want the big picture to make sense, begin with Christ.

- If it is not in writing, it does not exist.

- I speak blessings over your life.

- If you think twice before you speak once, you will speak twice the better for it.

- In all debates, let the truth be your aim, not victory or urgent interest.

- If God does not find you guilty, don't judge yourself.

- If you keep robbing your loved ones of time, there may come a day when they have no time for you.

- Instead of judging others, we should invest in our own mercy account. We will need it soon enough.

- If an engagement ring stays on a woman's finger for too long, it does not upgrade to a wedding, but it becomes a keyholder.

- Insanity has been defined as doing the same thing over and over again and hoping for different results. And there is wisdom in that.

- If you really, really, really believe that God is on your side, you will be optimistic even in the face of overwhelming obstacles and discouragement.

- If you want to change your feelings, change your focus.

- Instead of praying that God would allow you to lead others, pray for opportunities to serve others.

- If you want to know what is in a person's heart, listen to his or her words.

- It is better to keep your mouth shut and let the people think you are a fool than to open your mouth and remove all doubt.

- 'I am tired' is sometimes counterproductive.

- If you want your team to serve, serve them.

- If you want your people to care, care about them.

- If you want your employees to be their best, give them the best.

- It is unhealthy when we want all our good deeds to be known.

- It takes prayer, humility and patience to develop the right people.

- In God's kingdom, the power is at the bottom.

- If you want to meet people's needs, you have to be close and personal.

- It is easy to take salvation for granted.

- It is the Lord who provides answers, peace, hope and grace for every situation.

- If you immerse yourself in sacrifice, God speaks to you.

- It is God who gives insight into every situation.

- If you want true understanding, meditate on the scriptures always.

- If you are not bringing new ideas and information to the table on regular basis, people will start looking elsewhere.

- It is time to check what you are wearing – at the banquet he was not wearing the banquet gown (garment).

- Identify your weak spots and work on them.

- In heaven, we will be perfected and glorified.

- If Jesus has not touched you, you touch Him.

- Is your lifestyle touching Jesus? II Kings 20:1-6

- Is your giving touching Jesus? I Kings 17:7-15 widow's mite.

- I would rather walk with God in the dark than go alone in the light.

- It takes every part of the body working together to have a healthy body that functions properly.

- If you don't exercise your spiritual gifts, you hinder the ministry of your church.

- I am like a man fishing with my hands in a stream. I have caught a small fish in one, but a bigger fish is swimming by. To catch the bigger fish, I have to let go of the smaller one.

- If the Lord takes us to Heaven, it is His timing. But if not, we have another year on earth to live for Him.

- If you want to know how to pray in hard times, pray in the easy times.

- If you don't want the fruits of sin, stay out of the devil's orchard.

- In your desert of trials, Jesus will provide an oasis of Grace.

- It is a weak person who only serves God in times of blessing.

- It is God's grace that invites us to salvation, not out of our works or self-righteousness.

- If you 'make' disciples, you will always get a church. But if you are seeking to build the church, you rarely get disciples.

- It is time to come out of the wilderness into the promised land.

- "I cannot share you with God," said a churchgoer to a Christian sister he wants to marry – food for thought.

- If your life deviates from the screen, it does not change the screen but it changes you.

- If you want to go fast, go alone. If you want to go far, go together.

- In football, the one with the ball is the one who is tackled.

- In trading, you have to buy something before you can ask for extra (in Ghanaian dialect, "wo t) bia na wosre ntosoe")

- Innocence and purity before God caused the lions their appetite in Daniel's case.

- Inheritance got hastily at the beginning will not be blessed at the end – Prov. 20:21.

- It is impossible to change the direction of an anchored ship, but easy to change its direction once it is moving.

- If your conscience is programmed and governed by God's word, it will lead you to do the right things every time.

- If His grace touches your life, you will become a new being.

- If your mind is always on yesterday, you will be leaning in that direction.

- In the walk of faith, sometimes, you come to a sign that says, "Expect Delays".

- It is time to check what you are wearing.

- If you want to sell to John Smith what John Smith buys, you must see John Smith through John Smith's eyes.

- It is not about what God wants to do for you, but what He wants to do through you that will bless others.

REFLECTION

These strength-affirming aphorisms encourage thoughtful introspection and remind us of the spiritual principles that shape our daily lives. Whether they speak of discipline, trust, wisdom, or calling, they urge us to live with purpose and a godly perspective. Pause to reflect on how these truths may apply to your journey right now.

APHORISM

J

---

*Jesus is the lifeline to all
who are drowning in sin*

Ama stood at the edge of the bridge, staring into the black water below. It wasn't that she wanted to die—it was that she couldn't see a reason to live. Guilt had swallowed her after a series of reckless decisions: a broken family, a lost job, and shame that clung to her like a second skin.

She remembered the Sunday school songs from childhood, the prayers her mother used to whisper at her bedside. But that felt like another life.

Just as she took a trembling step forward, she heard a voice—real and urgent. 'Don't jump! Jesus loves you!' A man stood behind her holding a Bible, his voice shaking but full of compassion.

He introduced himself as Ofori, a street evangelist. 'I don't know why, but God told me to walk this route tonight. You're not alone. Jesus sees you, and He wants you to live.'

Tears spilt down Ama's cheeks. She stepped back from the ledge and collapsed into his arms, sobbing.

Ofori shared his own story—how he had once been deep in drugs and despair until Jesus pulled him out. 'He's not waiting for you to clean up. He's reaching out to rescue you now.'

That night, on a cold bench near the bridge, Ama surrendered her heart to Christ. It wasn't a dramatic glow or thunderous voice, just a peace she hadn't felt in years.

Today, Ama is a crisis counsellor, known for her soft voice and unshakable faith. She often tells clients:

'You may be drowning, but Jesus is still throwing lifelines. Grab hold. You're not too far gone for His grace.'

EXPLORE MORE APHORISMS

- Jesus is preparing a place for us and preparing us for that place.

- Jesus' resurrection spelt the end of death.

- Jesus alone can satisfy the empty space in your heart.

- Jesus knows your address.

- Jesus cares. He considers. He carries out His plan and it is always for your benefit.

- Jesus is on every page.

- Jesus purchased and offered to those who will receive Him into their lives Heaven.

- Jacob was a cheater, David had an affair, Noah got drunk, Peter had a temper, Jonah ran from God,

Paul was a murderer, Marian was gossiper, Gideon was insecure, Martha was a worrier, Thomas was a doubter, Sarah was impatient, Elijah was depressed, Zaccheus was short, Lazarus was dead and Abraham was old but God does not call the qualified. He qualifies the called.

- Jesus had a divine appointment with the Samaritan woman. Expect yours soon.

- Jesus, when you let Him go because of your sin, He will not let you go because of His grace.

- Jesus, give me eyes to see and ears to hear today, so that I can serve, even in a small way, the least of those who cross my path.

- Jesus will create good fruit in your life if you remain connected to Him.

- Jesus is not a knight in shining armour. He is the risen king of the ages.

- Jesus brought revelation to the Gentiles and glory to the people of Israel (Lk 2:32).

- Jesus may not show up when you want Him to but He will always show up on time so don't let your heart be troubled.

- Just as Christ Jesus was perfect and without sin, the lamb at the Passover was to be without blemish.

- Jeremiah Study Bible (JSB) says both hot and cold are good for the following reasons:

» The water from the hot spring of Hierapolis was useful for healing and restoration.

» The water at Colossae was refreshing to drink and quenched the thirst of the people.

» But the water that reached Laodicea was distasteful and unsatisfying (not cold, not hot, but lukewarm).

• Jesus provides an oasis of grace in the desert of trials.

• Jealousy can change a man into a leopard.

• Jesus let His own 'house' be torn down for the sake of your 'house' to stand.

REFLECTION

These aphorisms reveal profound truths about the people represented and the work of Jesus Christ. They offer comfort, conviction, or clarity about who He is and what He has done for us. Let these truths settle in your spirit today and renew your confidence in Christ's love and eternal plan for your life.

Aphorism

K

Keep your eyes on God.
He never takes His eyes off you

Yaw was a long-distance runner known for his discipline and focus. One day, he entered a race that wound through rough terrain and steep hills. The final leg of the course was a winding path uphill, with spectators cheering on both sides.

As Yaw approached the last stretch, he heard a voice call out, 'Your closest rival is catching up!' In a moment of panic, he looked back. His foot landed awkwardly on a stone, and he stumbled, nearly falling.

He regained his balance, but the rhythm was broken. He crossed the finish line second.

Later that evening, his coach pulled him aside. 'Yaw, you were leading. You had the pace. But the moment you took your eyes off your goal, you lost your momentum. Next time, eyes forward.'

That night, Yaw thought about his spiritual race. Life had been throwing distractions lately—financial stress, family pressure, and unanswered prayers. He realised he'd been glancing sideways at others and looking back at past failures.

He opened his Bible and read Hebrews 12:2: *"Let us fix our eyes on Jesus, the author and perfecter of our faith."* In that moment, he understood: spiritual success wasn't about outpacing others—it was about focusing solely on God.

From then on, Yaw prayed differently. 'Lord, keep me from comparing, complaining, or compromising. Just help me keep my eyes on You.'

He later shared this with his church youth group:

'God never blinks when it comes to you. He's always watching. The key is not whether He sees you—it's whether you're still looking at Him.'

EXPLORE MORE APHORISMS

- Keep your eyes on Jesus, and you will soon lose sight of your eyes.

- Know when to say nothing.

- Know when to say no.

- Kindness is the language the blind can see and the deaf can hear.

- Keep walking by faith and look for the morning of joy to come.

- King Saul succumbed to jealousy and wanted to kill David. How strong is your jealousy and where is it leading you?

- Knowledge says I have information and know what to do with it.

- Know your Bible. Satan took scriptures out of context to try to trap Jesus, but Jesus knew the context so did not fall for it.

- Keep doing what God has called you to do and leave the rest to Him.

- Know what to do and what not to do.

- Keep your marital secrets to yourself.

- Kindness is the best medicine.

REFLECTION

The aphorisms speak to the quiet disciplines of the Christian life—faith, wisdom, restraint, and love. They call us to focus on Jesus, walk in humility, and respond with discernment. Let them shape your responses and renew your devotion to the path of godly living.

Aphorism
L

Love is not a feeling;
it's a decision to act like Christ

Kate and Nkwatabisa had been married for ten years when the cracks began to show. The honeymoon glow had long faded, and everyday stress—kids, bills, unspoken frustrations—was taking its toll. Arguments replaced affection, and cold silence often lingered longer than apologies.

One evening, after a particularly bitter exchange, Kate sat alone in the kitchen, wiping tears off the table. She opened a devotional and read:

"But God demonstrates His own love for us in this: While we were still sinners, Christ died for us." (Romans 5:8)

She paused. Jesus didn't wait to feel love—He acted on it. And not when people were lovable, but when they were lost.

The next morning, she made a quiet decision. She brewed Nkwatabisa's coffee without being asked, left a note on his lunchbox, and hugged him goodnight even when her emotions hadn't caught up.

Nkwatabisa noticed. Slowly, the ice began to melt. He, too, chose love, initiating grace-filled conversations, apologising first, and praying with her.

Years later, Kate shared their journey with a young couple in crisis:

'Love won't always feel romantic. Sometimes it's a choice to wash feet when you feel like walking away. That's what Jesus did. And that's what saves marriages.'

EXPLORE MORE APHORISMS

- Life is designed for companionship, not isolation, for intimacy, not loneliness.

- Life is short-lived for God.

- Life is a gift from God to be lived for God.

- Learn from your failures or you will fail to learn.

- Love is more than a feeling; it is a commitment.

- Live better than what you preach.

- Love enables us to walk fearlessly, to run confidently and live victoriously.

- Life is a series of battles. Are you training to win?

- Living in the past paralyses the present and bankrupts the future.

- Little becomes much in the hands of Jesus (God).

- Let your emotions subside before you decide.

- Love is not love till you give it away.

- Light reveals righteousness and also reveals sin.

- "Lord, give me patience, and I want it now," is not the right kind of fruit of the Spirit.

- Listen to your father more than your feelings.

- Learn to move forward on your knees.

- Lot chose the wrong direction and lost. Abraham chose the right direction and won. Choices! Choices!!

- Life is in stages.

- Life is a cafeteria; you can get anything you want if you are willing to pay the price.

- Laughter is God's prescription for stress, so keep on laughing.

- Lepers were to keep their distance (II Kings 7:3) Covid-19, people were to keep their distance – coincidence?

- Logic and equation: If Eve=good and woman=Eve then good=woman; all women are good logically.

- Leaders must resist the temptation to be heroes.

- Let the wise listen and add to their learning and the discerning get guidance.

- Listen without interruption, that is, resist the temptation to jump in and finish the sentence or hijack the floor.

- Listen to understand the views of others, their feelings, thinking and needs.

- Listen but ask them to help get you on the same page with them.

- Life is full of issues; give yours to Christ Jesus, for He deals with issues.

- Let's dive deep, count our blessings, refine and use our spiritual tools and thank God daily for all his blessings, positional and practical.

- Little sins add up to big trouble.

- Love is a creative gift.

- Lions lost their appetite when Daniel was put in their den – Reason – Innocence and purity.

REFLECTION

The aphorisms offer compelling truths about how we are to live with purpose, love, and godly perspective. They challenge us to seek community, embrace responsibility, and navigate life's seasons with Christ at the centre. Let these truths guide you to honour God with the way you live, love, and lead.

APHORISM

M

Many want the crown, but not the cross

Agyeman had dreams of ministry success. From the day he preached his first sermon as a teenager, he envisioned crowds, conferences, and platforms. He admired the great preachers he saw online and believed he was called to do the same.

After Bible college, Agyeman was offered a small church in a rural village. No lights, no livestreams—just a few faithful elderly members and a leaky roof.

Frustrated, he asked God, 'Is this really where You want me?'

One day, an old farmer named Papa Tudah approached him after service. 'Son,' he said, 'you speak well. But can you suffer well? The crown shines, but the cross bleeds. Jesus carried the cross before He wore the crown.'

Those words echoed in Agyeman's heart. He began to pray differently—not for elevation, but for endurance. He visited the sick, served without applause, and preached as though he were speaking to thousands.

Years later, his ministry grew—not through gimmicks, but through faithfulness. He often told young leaders:

'Don't rush to be recognised. Be ready to be refined. If Jesus walked the road of sacrifice, so must we. Many want the crown—but the cross comes first.'

EXPLORE MORE APHORISMS

- Misunderstanding must be exposed before true understanding can flourish.

- Make sure that when you leave a person, he is closer to Jesus than when you first met him.

- Maturity means you don't have to say everything you think.

- Mothers are the best nurses (God intends mothers to be nurses).

- Maturity must precede prosperity.

- Many of us fail, not because we aren't talented, determined or passionate, but because we got 'side-tracked'.

- Making the right decision may come at a cost.

- Make failure your teacher, not your undertaker.

- Man's rejection is God's redirection.

- Make your one thing the main thing.

- Ministry means 'service', and to follow is to serve.

- Ministry begins when people start to follow Jesus – a hallmark of discipleship.

- Many of us have the self-control to start dieting or the program, but lack the perseverance, and therefore never cross the finish line.

- My son, listen to old counsel.

- May God give us wisdom to know when to work, serve and when to relax.

- Marriage was conceived and born in the mind of God.

- May the angels bring you Good News this Christmas.

- My Jesus helps you to fortify the weak places so that you might stand strong when the floods come.

- Made in heaven, not in any country, is the manna.

- May we be invigorated by the resurrection to share the good news with others as did Mary and Mary Magdalene.

- Marriage thrives in a climate of honour and respect.

- Make your plans and goals but submit them to God's guidance and He will direct your steps.

- Man-made religion always looks at the outside and condemns, but Christ Jesus always looks into the inside and forgives and cleanses.

REFLECTION

The aphorisms carry a message that invites intentionality in your walk with Christ. They address personal growth, spiritual maturity, and relational impact—cornerstones of a Christlike life. Let these truths inspire thoughtful action and deeper dependence on God's grace in your daily life.

APHORISM
N

Never doubt in the dark what
God told you in the light

Vida had always known she was called to missionary work. From her teenage years, God had stirred a fire in her heart for the unreached. After university, she joined a Christian NGO and moved to a remote village in northern Ghana to serve as a health worker and evangelist.

The early days were filled with joy—community outreach, testimonies, and late-night worship under the stars. But then came the hard days. Opposition from locals, spiritual attacks, and a sudden illness drained her strength. Prayer felt hollow. Silence replaced clarity.

One night, lying in a hospital bed miles away from home, Vida whispered through tears, 'Lord, did I make a mistake? Did You really send me here?'

Then she remembered a journal entry she'd written two years earlier. She'd penned the words: *"God said, 'Go.' I may not always understand the why, but I'll trust the Who."* That memory was a beam of light in her darkest valley.

Eventually, Vida recovered. She returned to the village, slower but surer. The fruit didn't come overnight, but it came—souls saved, hearts healed, a church planted.

Today, she often shares with young believers:

'Feelings fluctuate. Circumstances shift. But when God speaks in the light, hold fast when darkness comes. His promises don't expire in the storm.'

Explore more Aphorisms

- No evil can penetrate the armour of God.

- No legacy is as rich as integrity.

- No righteousness, no freedom.

- Nothing is stronger than the strength under God's control.

- Nothing surprises God.

- No life is more secure than a life surrendered to God.

- Nothing can stop progress if you are in the Will and Plan of God.

- Not a single material thing we possess in this life will be useful to us in the Eternal Age.

- Not all that you want is good for you.

- No man is so sick when he does not know he is sick.

- No wisdom in flogging a dead horse.

- Not everything in life has a logical explanation.

- Nothing is more important in life than the choices you make.

- No building on this earth lasts forever.

- Nothing in life is a sure bet except investments bearing an eternal dividend.

- No one is to appear before me empty-handed (Ex. 23:15b).

- Not losing sight of God in the midst of misfortune is one of the keys to survival.

- Nothing is too little to multiply in Jesus' hands.

- New Year's resolutions date back to the Babylonians who made vows to appease their gods, thinking the gods would make an unknown future secure. Jesus Christ, the same yesterday, today, and tomorrow (Heb. 13:8) can secure your future.

- No matter what life gives me. God can "put gladness in my heart (Ps 4:7)

- Nature forms us; sin deforms; school informs us; Christ transforms us.

- Never speak without thinking.

- New believers, like children, need loads of encouragement or else the enemy will work overtime to prevent their faith from flourishing.

REFLECTION

The aphorisms reflect deep spiritual truths about security, integrity, purpose, and God's sovereignty. They remind us to trust fully in God's protection, timing, and providence. Let these truths encourage steadfast faith and holy living.

APHORISM

O

Obedience is the bridge between revelation and manifestation

Obed, a carpenter in a quiet town, was known for his faith and simplicity. One night, during prayer, he felt the Lord impress on his heart: 'Build a prayer shed at the edge of the village. I will meet people there.' It sounded strange. No voice from heaven, no grand vision—just a quiet conviction.

He shared it with his wife. 'A prayer shed?' she asked, confused. 'Will anyone even come?' Obed shrugged. 'I don't know. But God said it.'

So he began. He used his savings, cleared land, and built a simple wooden hut with benches and an open Bible on the pulpit. Weeks passed. The shed sat empty.

Then one afternoon, a woman stumbled in crying. Her child had run away. She saw the sign outside, *"Come, all who are weary."* She poured out her heart and found peace. She brought others. Soon, every evening, the shed filled with villagers seeking God.

One day, a visiting missionary heard about it and offered support to plant a full church there. Obed wept. 'All I did was obey.'

He later told a gathering:

'God doesn't ask us to understand—only to obey. I had the revelation. But until I obeyed, there was no manifestation. Obedience built the bridge.'

EXPLORE MORE APHORISMS

- Our proof of our love for God is our love for our neighbour.

- Own up to your sin and experience the joy of confession.

- Our rough edges must be chipped away to bring out the image of Christ.

- Only God has the right to define what is wrong.

- Only Christ, the living water, can quench our spiritual thirst.

- One with God is the majority.

- Out of weakness, Jesus can reveal His strength.

- Out of the greatest tests come your greatest testimonies.

- Our eternity in heaven is secured through Christ.

- One preacher said the word Bible stands for Basic Instruction Before Leaving Earth.

- Our joy is not based on man's opinion.

- Our hope is not built on the approval rating of the public.

- Opportunity missed is opportunity lost.

- "Occupational hazard of a Christian ministry" is what John Scot called discouragement.

- One of the best ways to persuade others is by listening to them.

- Only Jesus opened the blind's eyes; not even the disciples or the apostles in the Bible did.

- Only in humble service are true leaders born.

- One of the surest signs of wisdom and maturity is the ability to say the right thing in the right way, at the right time for the right person.

- One of the surest signs of maturity is to say nothing at all.

- Only Jesus qualifies to throw the first stone

- Organisations that deliver the best service have a culture where employees are valued, listened to and cared for.

- Only Jesus knows his eternal origin and His divine mission.

- Our wisdom is folly unless we are following Christ.

- Only the fear of God can remove the fear of death.

- Our hearts are a battleground of continual conflict.

REFLECTION

The aphorisms invite deep reflection on how we relate to others, how we understand truth, and how we grow in grace. These insights are a call to humility, honesty, and holy living. Let these reflections prompt genuine spiritual transformation in how you live out your faith.

APHORISM
P

Prayer is the only power
that pulls down strongholds
without touching them

Pastor Boadu had been ministering in a spiritually resistant village for three years. Despite tireless outreach, home visits, and open-air crusades, the stronghold of ancestral worship seemed immovable. Every breakthrough was quickly met with opposition, and every conversion seemed to be followed by persecution.

One evening, weary and disheartened, he confided in his mentor. 'I've tried everything. Preaching. Fasting. Community service. Nothing is shifting.'

The mentor looked at him with compassion and said, 'Have you tried praying like it's your only strategy, not your backup plan?'

Conflicted, Pastor Boadu gathered his few church members and launched what he called "Night Watch"—a weekly prayer vigil specifically targeting spiritual strongholds.

They didn't confront village elders or protest rituals. They simply knelt in prayer, declaring God's authority over the land.

After six weeks, something shifted. A prominent priest's daughter came to a vigil and gave her life to Christ. Then the chief's wife was miraculously healed after a group fasted and prayed for her.

Slowly, hearts softened. Walls fell. Within a year, a church building was raised where sacrifices were once made.

At the church's dedication, Pastor Boadu preached just one message:

'We never fought in the flesh. We fought on our knees. And the strongholds fell—not because we touched them, but because God did.'

EXPLORE MORE APHORISMS

- Pray as if everything depends on God; work as if everything depends on you.

- Pray for the ability to see the world through Jesus' eyes.

- Pray for open doors, then look for them.

- Prayer does not change God, but it changes him who prays.

- Prayers, like eggs, don't hatch as soon as they are laid.

- Patience is a very slow-growing fruit that thrives best in soil of trials and troubles.

- People who are hurting often hurt other people so ask God for help if you are hurting.

- Personal experience and possessions dictate what we can attempt to pass on to others.

- Patience is simply trusting God with things like "why", "how" and "when".

- Problems reveal the power of God in us.

- Preaching is the chariot that carries Christ up and down the world.

- Paul's treatment of Onesimus created new ways of looking at slaves.

- Preaching has authority only when the message comes as a word from God Himself.

- Pick your battles wisely, and don't waste time on the unimportant.

- Praise stirs emotions, Praise rubs off and it is contagious.

- Put God first and everything else will follow.

- Pray for God to bring your hunger for fame and recognition under control.

- Parents show their children they are valued by lovingly caring for them.

- Positional blessings in Christ never change, but Practical blessings of the righteous living change – they need the attention and discernment to walk faithfully and fruitfully with Christ.

- Personal growth won't happen if you don't take responsibility.

- Prayer moves the hand that moves the world.

- Peter denied Jesus but Jesus did not deny him.

- People are not illegal. Their status may be irregular, but that does not render them beyond humanity (By Nils Muiznicks) – The Council of Europe's Human Rights Commissioner.

- Pay the price to get the prize.

REFLECTION

The aphorisms encourage a faith that is both active and anchored in God. They speak to the vital role of prayer, responsibility, perspective, and perseverance on the Christian journey. Let them remind you to trust in God's timing and to be faithful in both prayer and practice.

APHORISM

Q

Quality is judged by the customer,
not the organisation—and first
impressions always count

Quansah had just been appointed the welcome team leader at his local church. Passionate and full of ideas, he launched into rebranding their welcome booth—new signage, matching shirts, and better snacks.

But one Sunday, a quiet teenage boy named Adotey came alone. He hovered near the church gate, unsure whether to enter. The ushers were busy discussing logistics, and no one noticed him.

Eventually, Adotey turned away. That week, the pastor received a message from Adotey's aunt: 'He came seeking hope after battling depression. But he didn't feel seen.'

Quansah was crushed. He prayed, fasted, and re-evaluated everything. The next Sunday, he trained his team with a new mindset: 'We're not welcoming visitors. We're representing Christ. To them, we *are* the Church.'

He began to focus not just on hospitality, but on the heart. They made eye contact, learned names, and followed up with personal calls. Slowly, the culture shifted.

Months later, Adotey returned. This time, Quansah greeted him personally. They talked. Prayed. Adotey stayed.

Today, he's part of the youth choir. When asked what changed, he says: 'The Church stopped being a place I walked into. It became a people who walked up to me.'

Quansah often reminds his team: 'Your quality isn't what you say about yourselves—it's what the hurting say after encountering you. So make every impression count.'

EXPLORE MORE APHORISMS

- Quality is judged by the customer not the organisation and first impressions always count.

- Quiet time with God fuels a noisy world.

- Questions are the beginning of revelation.

- Quitters never witness the miracle.

- Quick fixes often cause long delays.

- Quality friendships are forged in truth and tested in trials.

- Quiet obedience is louder in heaven than public display.

- Qualified by grace, not by résumé.

- Quenching the Spirit begins with small compromises.

- Quick to listen, slow to speak, slower to take offence.

- Quiet waters run deep; so does steady faith.

REFLECTION

Quality in the Kingdom is not defined by what we claim about ourselves but by the testimony others carry after encountering us. As Christ's ambassadors, our first impressions may become someone's first glimpse of Jesus. Every handshake, every word, every act of kindness is an opportunity to reveal His love. Let these truths remind you that excellence is not about perfection but about reflecting Christ's heart with sincerity and care in every interaction.

APHORISM
R

Remember, the road to
hell is smooth and straight;
it takes no effort to get there

Adusei was a good man by society's standards. He paid his taxes, donated to charities, and always offered a helping hand. He believed that as long as he wasn't hurting anyone, he'd be fine with God. Church? Occasionally. Bible? Rarely. Prayer? Only in crisis.

One day, an old friend invited him to a revival meeting. Adusei politely declined. 'I don't need religion to be moral,' he said. 'I'm living right.'

But that night, he couldn't sleep. A line from a podcast he'd half-listened to haunted him: *"The path to hell is often paved with good intentions."*

He finally agreed to attend the last night of the revival. The preacher told a parable: two men walking down a beautiful path lined with flowers and ease, only to find it led to destruction. Another man took a narrow, thorny road filled with trials— but it ended in glory.

'Hell is not reserved for monsters,' the preacher said, 'but for those who never accepted the invitation to life. The wide road requires no repentance, no surrender—just passive drifting.'

Adusei sat frozen. He realised he had been coasting through life without ever confronting his need for a Saviour.

That night, he came forward, tears in his eyes. 'I've been walking without Jesus. Today, I choose the narrow path.'

Years later, as a deacon in his church, Adusei tells new believers:

'Don't mistake comfort for safety. The wide road requires nothing of you—but it costs you everything in the end.'

Explore more Aphorisms

- Remember that part of the success of your past will be measured by what you do with it now and how well you use it to prepare for the future.

- Remember that what seems urgent may not in fact be important.

- Realise that rough times won't last forever.

- Reservation in heaven is still open, don't delay.

- Read the Word, say the Word and live by the Word if you want to grow in your Christian journey.

- Relief began with confession to God and accepting the forgiveness He offers.

- Remember God's goodness to you in the past and you will be revived.

- Repentance is simply the right response to wrong living.

- Remember, the simplicity of Christianity is its difficulty

- Reading the Bible convicts, inspires and helps us to live for God, for it guides us into the truth (II Tim. 2:15).

- Revival gives new freshness to us.

- Right thinking leads to right living.

- Remember, if you trust, you don't worry, and if you worry, you don't trust.

- Relationships come in all shapes and sizes.

- Religious acts are doing all Christian activities without Christ living in you.

- Remember, with Jesus in the boat, the Breakdown will change to Breakthrough.

- Remember, salvation is God's free gift to man.

- Remember, your 'Garden of Eden' will surely come to pass.

- Remember the first fear – fear entered the hearts of Adam and Eve as they thought of meeting God so they hid themselves among the trees in the garden.

- Right is right, even if nobody does it and wrong is wrong even if everybody does it.

- A recently married man must not go to war (Deut. 24:5).

- Remain connected to Jesus to bear fruit.

REFLECTION

The aphorisms draw attention to perspective, preparation, and priority in our walk of faith. They challenge us to reflect on how we manage our time, apply God's Word, and invest in eternity. Let them encourage intentional living and remind you of heaven's values over earth's distractions.

Aphorism
S

Satan trembles when he sees the weakest saint upon his knees

Salome was a quiet woman in her seventies, rarely noticed in church beyond her gentle smile and well-worn Bible. She walked slowly, spoke softly, and rarely stood at the pulpit. But unknown to most, she was the spiritual engine room of the church.

Every morning at 4 a.m., Salome would wake up, light a small candle by her bedside, and begin to pray. She called it her 'war room.' Names of missionaries, church leaders, prodigal sons, broken marriages, and entire nations were scribbled in her tattered notebook.

One Sunday, a young pastor named Daniel was invited to preach. Nervous and insecure, he arrived early and prayed alone in the sanctuary. He didn't know Salome was in the back pew, silently interceding.

That day, revival broke out. Lives were changed. Healing flowed. The presence of God was tangible.

After the service, Daniel approached the senior pastor, overwhelmed. 'What happened today? I've never experienced anything like it.'

The pastor smiled and pointed toward the back: 'Ask Mama Salome. She's been praying for this day for ten years.'

Daniel sat beside her and said, 'You must be a mighty woman of God.' She smiled and whispered, 'No. I'm just weak enough to kneel and trust the One who is strong.'

Years later, Daniel would share her story across churches and say:

'The devil fears a praying saint more than a shouting preacher. Because the real battle is won on your knees, not on the stage.'

EXPLORE MORE APHORISMS

- Sin adds to your trouble, subtracts from your energy and multiplies your difficulties.

- Someday, the scales of justice will be perfectly balanced.

- Stories from the past can give us pointers for the present.

- Spiritual inactivity corrodes the souls.

- Start where you are serving the Lord; He will use your efforts to further His plan (By Anon).

- Say thank you to Jesus for not walking by when you were hurting, but for stopping to invite you into friendship with Him.

- Stop fighting God, for you will lose.

- Salvation is a gift that cannot be earned.

- Salvation is free and a gift but until you accept it, it is not yours.

- Sometimes God says "No" to our prayers because we "ask amiss".

- Sometimes your greatest blessings come from your most negative circumstances.

- Sacrifice to satisfy.

- Sometimes we let our failures define us.

- Some things just don't make sense until you experience them.

- Sometimes there is a long gap between promise and fulfilment.

- Some people don't know the value of the things they have until they lose them.

- Sometimes, trials, obstacles, difficulties and defeat are the very food of faith.

- Samson disobeyed God, squandered his opportunities and undermined his own power, yet he did not realise God had left him.

- Spiritual things control physical things so enter into the spiritual realm through prayer.

- Sometimes you have to shut the door.

- Share your problems with a trusted friend, for a problem shared is a problem halved.

- Stop running (Gen 16:8-9).

- Saying the right thing is important at the right time.

- Stop worrying about what you cannot do and start doing what you can do.

- Success is not in the absence of challenges; it is having the wisdom to manage them and keep moving forward.

- Self-control gets the footballer out of bed in the morning, but perseverance finishes the routine today, tomorrow and the next day.

- Surviving life's trials requires faith that is focused on our God, faith that enables us to say with Job and others, "May the name of the Lord be praised".

- Silence is wisdom, where speaking is folly.

- Speak what is fit, and when it is fit to speak.

- Salvation without discipleship is cheap.

- Sometimes God lets us take the longer route in life's careers or other endeavours, so that we will be better prepared for the journey ahead.

- Satan's favourite weapon is discouragement.

- Sometimes the wisest words are the ones never spoken.

- Set aside at least one day in a week to rest, spend time with your loved ones and fellowship with your church family.

- Submitting to God's guidance leads to stability and fruitfulness.

- Silence sometimes has a voice.

- Serving the Lord does not exempt us from life's storms, but it protects us when we are in them.

- Spouses show their mates that they are appreciated by listening to them and loving them.

- Sometimes God lets you reach the end of your rope in order to show you that you have nothing left but Him; He is all you need.

- Sometimes God sets us apart in order to prepare us for what is coming next. There is always a purpose in His plans.

- Some of us are verbal and others are quiet. Some of us are leaders and others are followers. Some have a high profile and others are inconspicuous.

- Since the Holy Spirit decides which particular gift each of us receives, there is no place for jealousy and competitiveness.

- Spiritual gifts are supernatural and endowments that enable us to carry out God's will in God's way.

- Successful people have different talents but they all have these qualities – perseverance, tenacity, and "stick-to-itiveness".

- Surrender means victory when we surrender to God.

- Sin is a disease; Christ is the cure.

- Sometimes the best witness is kindness.

- Sweet words do not take the place of food.

- Sometimes the devil magnifies the few problems you have above the many blessings you enjoy.

- Some secrets are meant to follow us to the grave, just for peace to reign.

- Sin causes fear.

- Share your love by telling what the Lord has done for you.

REFLECTION

The aphorisms challenge us to walk faithfully, persevere through trials, and remain spiritually active. They urge us to live with wisdom, grace, and purpose as we represent Christ in a broken world. Let them prompt you to evaluate your habits, renew your passion for God, and trust His justice and timing.

APHORISM

T

The true test of character is not how you act when things go well, but how you react when they go wrong

Thomas was the most celebrated employee in his company—known for his punctuality, professionalism, and results. But one day, a system error incorrectly flagged his name in a major scandal. Overnight, he was suspended and shamed. His inbox dried up, friends distanced themselves, and headlines whispered his guilt.

He was angry. Not just at the company, but at God. 'Why me? After all I've done with integrity?'

But instead of lashing out, Thomas took a different posture. He fasted. He prayed. And he forgave.

A few days later, a junior colleague who had remained silent came forward and confessed to the IT manager. The evidence was reviewed and cleared Thomas completely. The CEO personally apologised and offered him his position back—with a promotion.

At the next board meeting, Thomas stood and said: 'I'm grateful for my name being cleared. But more than that, I'm grateful for the trial. Because what was tested wasn't my reputation—it was my reaction. And by God's grace, I chose peace over pride.'

From that day, he became a sought-after mentor, not because of his success, but because of his serenity in suffering.

As he often told others: 'Storms don't build character. They reveal it. And when all goes wrong, that's when who you really are shows up.'

EXPLORE MORE APHORISMS

- Tiny evils big fall.

- The right kind of fear prompts us to do right.

- To conquer your fears, surrender them to the Lord.

- Those who have questions about Christ need someone who has the answers.

- To have more pray more.

- The most powerful testimony is a godly life.

- To choose Christ now is a choice for eternity.

- The search for forgiveness ends when you find Christ

- Two cannot quarrel when one will not.

- To ignore the Bible is to invite disaster.

- There is no place or time we cannot pray.

- To be anxious about nothing, pray about everything.

- The way of obedience is the way of blessing.

- The God who loves us knows our "expiration date".

- To get better with age, get spiritually fit.

- The next person you meet may need to meet Christ.

- The more you meditate on the scripture the closer you will be walking with the Saviour.

- The most deadly sins do not leap on us; they creep up on us.

- The first step in repenting from sin is to admit that you are to blame.

- The written Word reveals the living Word.

- The Good News of Christ is too good to keep to yourself. The wise will recognise their limitations and God's unlimited.

- The seed we sow today determines the kind of fruit we will reap tomorrow.

- To show His love, Jesus died for me; to show my love, I must live for Him.

- The income of God's Word is the Outcome of a changed life.

- The past is an important part of today's actions and tomorrow's plan (Hezekiah's profile).

- Time and distance are irrelevant in the spirit world.

- The past affects your decisions and actions today, and these in turn affect your future.

- There are lessons to learn and errors to avoid repeating from the past.

- The disgrace of okro is to the shame of cassava.

- The simplicity of Christianity is its difficulty.

- Tithing is not the last word in generosity; it is the first word (John Ortberg).

- Time is the most valuable commodity in life and how you spend it says something about you.

- The New Community of Heaven not only means every tear is wiped away forever, it also means there will be no death forever and ever.

- Those who guard their lips preserve their lives.

- There are no coincidences when we are in the "will of God" – His timing is perfect.

- There are no coincidences in our lives, only God's providence.

- There is strength in numbers, for though one may be overpowered, two can defend themselves.

- Together, we can stand firm when life's headwinds gust our way.

- To blow out your birthday candles means you are subtracting from the years God has given you.

- The failures of yesterday become today's success.

- Today's success becomes tomorrow's failure.

- Trust the One who hangs the earth on nothing (Job 26:7) to meet your needs.

- Take it step by step, day by day and moment by moment and you will reach your final destination.

- To grow spiritually, you need the 'strong meat' of God's word.

- Tough times don't last but tough people do.

- The heart of the prudent acquires knowledge and the ear of the wise seeks knowledge (Prov. 18:15).

- There came Pharaoh who did not know Joseph.

- The miracle of multiplication did not take place when the food left Christ's hands but the disciples' hands.

- The goodness of God leads to repentance (Rom. 2:4 NKJV).

- The measure of our spirituality is the amount of praise and thanksgiving in our prayers.

- The more spiritual we are, the more we shall think about heaven.

- The type of habits you have determines your character.

- There is no shortcut when it comes to perseverance.

- The word for you this week is – May the joy of the Lord become your strength.

- To mourn is to sympathise.

- There is no mistake Jesus cannot mend and no wound He cannot heal.

- The devil's activities come to a halt when Divine protection visits your house.

- The best way to learn to trust God in the present is to study His works from the past.

- The wicked may plot to harm you, but God will give His angels a divine assignment over you.

- Trim the hedge around your spiritual life so that you can enjoy pure, unadulterated followship with the King.

- The age of Methuselah has nothing to do with the wisdom of Solomon.

- The way to cover our sin is to uncover it by confession.

- The strength of what we believe is measured by how much we are willing to suffer for those beliefs.

- There is no way of obtaining favour from God but through the intercession of Christ.

- The most daunting tomorrow is no match for our God so move forward and God will meet you there.

- There is one central problem with looking back: the past cannot be changed.

- Turn your forward into forever.

- Teach your children about Sin.

- The neighbour laws were just one of the ways in which Israel was to be 'holy' like her God.

- The work which His goodness began, the arm of His strength will complete.

- Tough words hurt.

- The get-rich-quick mentality is not scriptural.

- This play-it-wise approach is not a play-it-safe approach.

- The gospel cannot be properly understood as good news without the preaching of the Law.

- The straight path is the cross.

- True love is always costly.

- Trees are connected to their roots, enabling them to flourish. Christians should also hold fast and deep to the Saviour for them to thrive and flourish too.

- The Bible story begins in a garden and ends in a city, the future city of God which will be the eternal home of Christ's people.

- The Lord makes your tomorrow better than today, this week better than last week and next month better than this month.

- The next time I see you, it is going to be better than today.

- The woman gave Peter and others the wrong address; be careful before you too give the wrong address of Jesus to people.

- The truth is, sometimes the more you speak, the less people remember.

- The difference between where you are right now and where you want to be can be summed up in two words – hard work!

- The law of reciprocity guarantees you will get back what you give. It is not a threat; it is an immutable law.

- There are no lost letters in heaven.

- Think about the worst kind of judging, judging the sins God has already forgiven and forgotten (Isa. 43:25).

- The guilt of our sin need not be permanent.

- There is a God whose arms open wide to receive us when we acknowledge our wrongs and seek His forgiveness.

- The shortest way is not always the best.

- The word hallelujah is a command form of the word "praise". It is an expression of worship, but it is also an order to start praising the Lord.

- The Israelites rejected God's prescription of marriage, so Moses gave them permission for divorce (Prescription vs permission).

- The mercy and grace in Jesus Christ brought about forgiveness.

- The gift of marriage became the crown jewel in God's creation.

- To move towards Jesus calls for waiting upon Him in prayer, Bible study, quiet time and trust.

- There is no joy in the world like the joy of bringing one soul to Christ.

- The peacemaker is significant because of its harvest.

- The guidebook to heaven is the Bible.

- Train people who can train others.

- Take time to listen and care.

- The hallmark of a Christian is love and you cannot love in a hurry.

- The bottom line is, if you sow, you will reap what you have sown.

- True humility serves quietly and finds satisfaction in serving.

- Thankfulness is a soil in which pride does not easily grow.

- To miss God's will is to miss the purpose for which you were born.

- True understanding comes from God; it is a gift only He can give.

- There is no emotion so deeply rooted that God's grace cannot reach down and remove it.

- The man who lost the gift of speech – Zachariah (Lk. 1:20).

- The cross shows us who we are, those whom God so loved that He gave His only Son for us (Jn. 3:16).

- Times of blessing in life are often followed by times of testing.

- They were saved by the blood of the sacrificial lamb (Ex. 12:26-27).

- There is always a starting point and a stopping point. Nothing lasts forever in humans (in this world).

- This year does not have to be like last year for you.

- The Lord is my inheritance, what about you?

- The fewer the pounds we have, the more careful our spending.

- To accept Jesus as your personal saviour will not cost you a penny, so hurry.

- There is a difference between position and condition.

- There are different gifts because there are different needs.

- The secret to success is not just in activity but in abiding in Him.

- The same wind that blew at your back on your way to hell, will blow in your face on your way to heaven.

- The Lord wants us to be cold – that is refreshing and thirst-quenching. He wants us to be hot – that is therapeutic and useful but never be lukewarm for Him.

- The price of growth is always less than the cost of ignorance and stagnation.

- The greatest obstacle to personal growth is the illusion of knowledge, not ignorance.

- The contented person is never poor; the discontented person is never rich.

- Trusting God's faithfulness dispels our fearfulness.

- To guide your children in the right way, you must go that way yourself.

- To understand the word of God, rely on the Spirit of God.

- The state of your heart determines the look on your face.

- Talk is cheap. It is easy to say we are devoted to Christ, but our claims are meaningful only when they are tested in the crucible of persecution.

- The Bible is the only book whose author is always present when it is read.

- The mind is formed by what it takes in.

- The best way to escape temptation is to run to God.

- Temptation always begins in the mind, and in order to protect it, we have to dwell on God's word.

- The key to failure is trying to please everybody.

- Trust is a fundamental feature of economic life.

- There is nothing more dangerous than half-knowledge.

- The glory of young men is their strength and the beauty of old men is their grey hair (Prov. 20:29).

- There must be a balance between your praises and your petitions.

- The good news is that it is not too late to allow God to use you.

- The 'coat' message shouted, "Joseph is my beloved son."

- There were many widows in Israel but God sent Elijah to the widow of Zarephath.

- There were many lepers in Israel but it was Naaman whom Elijah healed.

- Turn to God for strength as the days are evil.

- The devil's orchard is full of fruits of sin.

REFLECTION

The aphorisms offer guidance, warnings, or encouragement needed in navigating Christian life. They may point to faith, fear, truth, or perseverance—each calling us back to dependence on God's wisdom and grace. Take these truths to heart and ask the Lord how to live them out with greater conviction today.

APHORISM

U

---

*Until the pain of remaining
the same is greater than the
fear of change, transformation
will not happen*

Eunice had lived with bitterness for most of her adult life. A friend's betrayal in university had scarred her so deeply that she built emotional walls, refusing to let anyone in. Even at church, she smiled politely but kept her heart guarded.

For years, her pastor taught on forgiveness and healing, but she quietly nodded without ever applying it. Deep down, she feared that letting go meant becoming vulnerable again.

Then, one morning, she woke up unable to move her right arm. The doctors said it was a stress-induced muscular condition—something her grief and internal strain had triggered over time.

In the silence of recovery, Eunice heard the Holy Spirit whisper: 'You're not in pain because of what happened—you're in pain because you've refused to heal.'

That was her turning point. The pain of holding on had finally outweighed the fear of letting go.

She began counselling. She wrote a letter of forgiveness she never intended to send. And for the first time, she cried in prayer, tears that cleansed.

Months later, her health improved. Her relationships blossomed. And when asked what changed, she simply said:

'Change didn't begin with strength. It began with surrender. I stayed the same for too long because I feared change. But when the pain of staying broke me, God began to rebuild me.'

EXPLORE MORE APHORISMS

- Unless God reveals Himself, we cannot find Him. He reveals Himself in four ways: Through Creation, through the Prophets, through the Bible and above all through Jesus Christ.

- Unwise, ungodly counsel can lead to unseen dangers and be costly.

- Until you are free to die, you are not free to live.

- Until a "learning pill" is developed, the old-fashioned approach will have to do.

- Until you take the first step, you will remain stuck.

- Unforgiveness locks you to the past, drop it, leave it and let it go.

- Unconfessed sin can cause us serious spiritual agony.

REFLECTION

The aphorisms urge us to walk in divine wisdom and spiritual freedom. They remind us that revelation, growth, and healing come through God's initiative and our humble response. Let them inspire you to take the necessary steps of faith and let go of anything hindering your walk with Christ.

APHORISM
V

---

*Victory doesn't come from
the absence of battles but
from the presence of God
in the midst of them*

Buruwaa had just been diagnosed with breast cancer. She was a worship leader, a mother of two, and the pillar of her women's fellowship. But the news hit her like a flood. She wasn't afraid to die—she was afraid to suffer.

Everyone around her expected her to be strong. They quoted verses, sent songs, and declared healing. But Buruwaa wrestled quietly. 'God, where are You in this fight?'

One night, after her second chemotherapy session, Buruwaa sat alone at church, too weak to stand, too tired to cry. In the silence, she felt a warmth flooding her chest. No voice. No vision. Just the unmistakable peace of God's presence.

From that moment, everything changed—not her diagnosis, but her posture. She began documenting her journey, singing even when her hair fell out, smiling even when pain came.

People started joining her hospital room for worship. Nurses cried. Patients asked questions. Her battle became a ministry.

After her final treatment, the doctor said, 'You've fought well.' Buruwaa replied, 'I didn't win because the cancer left, I won because God never did.'

To this day, she testifies:

'Victory isn't the storm ending. It's knowing Who is in the boat with you while it rages.'

EXPLORE MORE APHORISMS

- Vex money, do the youth (girls) go out with some?

- View yourself as belonging to God not yourself.

- Victory goes to the man or woman who is willing to fight one more round. When you quit, God can do no more for you. But when you persevere, He will come to your aid.

REFLECTION

The aphorisms invite us to reflect on identity, perseverance, and our values. Each phrase challenges worldly assumptions and reorients our thinking toward spiritual truth and godly endurance. Let them sharpen your focus and reignite your resolve to keep pressing forward in faith.

APHORISM
W

*Worry is a conversation
you have with yourself about
things you cannot change.
Prayer is a conversation with
God about the things He can*

Angelina had always been a planner. Lists, calendars, backup plans—she liked to be in control. So, when her husband lost his job unexpectedly, her world tilted. The mortgage, their son's school fees, medical bills—it all piled up in her mind like bricks.

She stopped sleeping. She stopped laughing. Her Bible gathered dust while her journal filled with anxious entries. One morning, she read back through her notes and noticed something: every page ended with a question mark, never a prayer.

That Sunday, her pastor preached on Philippians 4:6—*"Do not be anxious about anything, but in everything, by prayer and petition, with thanksgiving, present your requests to God."*

It hit her like thunder. She realised she'd been talking to herself about her problems instead of talking to God.

That night, she knelt down and poured everything out. Every fear. Every doubt. Every bill. No poetry—just honesty. Then she got up, lighter.

Two weeks later, her husband got a contract. Unexpected funds came through a delayed refund. Peace slowly replaced panic.

Now, whenever someone says, 'I'm worried,' Angelina gently replies:

'Worry keeps you circling the problem. Prayer takes you to the Problem-Solver. Stop rehearsing the chaos—start releasing it to Christ.'

EXPLORE MORE APHORISMS

- When God gives an assignment, it comes with His enablement.

- When we forget our priorities, we argue about trivialities.

- When telling others what Christ can do for them, tell them what He has done for you.

- Where God's finger points, His hand will make a way.

- When God wipes our tears, sorrow gives way to eternal song.

- We honour God when we honour our leaders.

- We don't have to wait in line, enter a building or wear nice clothing to talk to God.

- When God shows you a problem, He may ask you to be His solution.

- When troubles call on you, you call on God.

- What you will become tomorrow depends on the choices you make today.

- When you open your heart to the Saviour, He opens your mind to His word.

- When Jesus comes into a life, He changes everything.

- When God forgives, He removes our sin and restores our souls.

- Work for God done well will receive God's "well done".

- Wise is the person who knows what to say and when to say it.

- We are saved not by what we do but by trusting what Christ has done.

- We can face any fear when we know the Lord is near.

- When we open our hearts to the Lord, He opens our eyes to the Lost.

- When we draw near to God, our minds are refreshed and our strength is renewed.

- We can never sacrifice too much for him who sacrificed His all for us.

- When money, status, wealth, fame and occupation all fail, try Jesus.

- What is OK in private may not be in public.

- When God is the source of your vision, He will resource it.

- Worry is like a "No-Confidence" in God.

- Without a plan for your life, life just 'happens' to you.

- When things don't happen on our schedule or to our expectations, we must submit our plans to God and walk by faith.

- Wisdom teaches us what to do with knowledge.

- We need relationships with each other for encouragement, refreshment and growth.

- When we put our heads on the pillow at night, we should pause to thank God for the amazing things he has done for us that day in the midst of our ordinary lives.

- What peace can they have who are not at peace with God?

- We are saved 'for good works' after we are saved by grace.

- When God calls you to wrestle with Him in prayer, it is an invitation to receive His blessing.

- Water and oil are more compatible than Christianity and prejudice.

- When the Red letters of Jesus Christ become the Read letters of Jesus, our soul is enriched.

- When you knowingly don't please God, He will stop blessing you.

- When you know you have heard from God, the criticism of others will affect you less.

- When you demonstrate maturity, you can go to God with confidence.

- We learn by listening and observing.

- When Justice and Mercy meet together, Grace is the end product.

- While you are sleeping, someone is awake.

- We would all like to be remembered for our "finest hour".

- Wisdom opens the eyes both to the glories of heaven and to the hollowness of the earth.

- When Grace and Mercy meet, the Heavens' windows are open.

- What you think produces how you feel.

- When righteousness is your goal, open doors are not far away.

- Weeping is often therapeutic but in Heaven there will be no weeping at all.

- Will you be at a battlefield with your soldiers or stay home and watch women taking a bath?

- When Grace, Mercy and Love attend to your needs, tears turn to laughter, sadness to joy and death to life.

- When Mercy and Grace pay you a visit, salvation is the end result.

- Weeping may endure for a night, but joy comes in the morning (Ps. 30:5).

- We are blessed when we let ourselves identify with the pain of others, feeling their sorrow, praying for their needs and lifting up their spirits.

- With God's mercy at work in our hearts and the hearts of others, we can forgive as He has forgiven us.

- Woe to the Christian who loves only the soft (inside) part of the doughnut.

- We live far below the level God intended because we see ourselves in the wrong light.

- Worship is a way of life.

- With God on your side, there is no enemy that can defeat you.

- When you are connected to the Vine, God's goodness and mercy will follow you all the days of your life.

- When the written Word became the Spoken Word, and the Spoken Word became the Living Word, death gave way to life, curse gave way to blessing, and sadness gave way to joy, tears gave way to laughter and weakness gave way to strength.

- When you receive a divine visitation, count it a blessing.

- Women are moved by what they hear and men are moved by what they see.

- Wives submitting and not mastering and husbands loving and not ruling.

- Whoever knows the God of the Old Testament, meets Him again in the New Testament with no transition adjustment necessary.

- We will have some bad days, but that is where faith comes in.

- When God has a job to be done, He calls a man or a woman to do it.

- When praise is directed towards God, stay out of the way.

- What goes around comes around – that is a timeless principle.

- When we judge others, we are looking in the wrong direction. We are avoiding what we don't want to see – our own shortcomings.

- Without risk, there is no reward.

- We forget for a lot of reasons:

  » The passage of time

  » When we are growing older

  » Just being too busy

- We forget passwords, names of people or even where we parked our car. This tells us that we are human after all.

- When things don't seem to happen quickly enough, we can trust in God, the one who leads and guides us.

- When you get discouraged, don't give up on our goals; instead, devise a new approach.

- When Satan brings discouragement to your door, don't open the door. Don't invite him in. Don't accept the package. Don't sign the receipt. Submit to God and resist him.

- Winners sacrifice the present for the future.

- Winners say no to indulgence and yes to discipline because to them, the prize is worth the price.

- Winners recognise that talent alone is not enough; you need a plan to live by.

- What is down in the well always comes up in the bucket.

- We pick our ticket to heaven when we are born again through faith in Jesus.

- With Christ Jesus in the boat, we can smile at the storm

- Wonder-working God, I hand over this battle to you and I trust in Your strength and promises, should be your cry.

- We don't have to live condemned when we make mistakes.

- We are sent to do God's will, not our own.

- Willingness and capability both come from God, not you.

- When your joy and peace seem to be gone, check your believing; usually it is gone also. Start believing and you will be restored.

- Which of Jesus' titles from Isaiah 9:6 means the most to you today and why?

- What took place on that Summit was a transaction between Father and Son alone (Genesis 22:7-8). The same event that took place on Mount Calvary (Golgotha) was between Father and Son alone (Matthew 27:46).

- We never realised the joy of our salvation until we found ourselves without that joy.

- When you know God has heard your prayer, anxiety is replaced with peace.

- Why are you going back to Egypt?

- We are careful about how we live when we are approaching the end of our lives.

- When you look inside yourself, you find your inadequacy. When you look around to God, you find that He is able to do exceedingly abundantly above all that we ask or think.

- We don't have a High Priest who is untouchable, but a touchable High Priest, so do touch him.

- We need some repairs to be done in our lives, so let's follow Jesus the repairer.

- When you touch God, you move God.

- What is important is that you have somewhere quiet with Him and meditate on his word.

- We serve God not by our own abilities but by depending upon the indwelling power of His Spirit.

- When life gets you down, keep looking up.

- We can get information online, but wisdom comes from on high.

- When you choose to rejoice, life takes on a beautiful colour.

- We don't need more to be thankful for; we need to be more thankful.

- When circumstances yield discouragement, I can still eat from God's rich banquet table of love.

- We can be spiritually strong in Christ, even when we are physically weak.

- When words become weapons, our relationships become casualties.

- We are saved to serve.

- We cannot only be good; we must be good for something.

- When we yield ourselves to the Lord and He works through us, the work goes faster and further than we realise.

- Worrying brings nothing; faith in God brings provision.

- When you come into contact with Jesus, you will never be the same.

- Winners are not only those who never fail but also those who never quit.

- We don't find friends, we make friends.

- Without the cross, there is no hope, and without the root, no fruits.

- What was raised was what was buried.

- When the Lord's blessing is upon what you have, you will succeed in spite of the challenges and obstacles.

- When your enemies try to use situations to destroy you, God can use them to develop you.

- When people and circumstances rule, God overrules.

REFLECTION

The aphorisms offer wisdom for living with faith, integrity, and courage. Whether they speak to divine calling, purpose, trials, or trust, they remind us that God is actively at work in our lives. Let them move you to trust more deeply, serve more faithfully, and live more purposefully under His direction.

APHORISM

Y

*You may be the only Bible
some people will ever read*

James worked in a busy accounting firm where open faith conversations were rare. He never preached at his colleagues, but he was always calm under pressure, quick to forgive, and generous with his time. People noticed.

One afternoon, a coworker named Lucy knocked on his office door. 'I need to ask you something,' she said. 'Are you a Christian?'

'Yes,' he replied gently. 'Why do you ask?'

Tears welled in her eyes. 'Because I've been watching you. The way you treated the intern who made a mistake, how you stayed back to help the janitor during the flood, how you pray before eating—it's different. And I want what you have.'

James was stunned. He had never quoted Scripture at work, yet somehow the gospel had been read through his life.

They began meeting weekly for coffee and prayer. Lucy eventually gave her life to Christ and later told a group: 'I used to think Christians were just religious people with rules.

But then I met someone who *lived* the love, peace, and grace I'd only heard about. He never preached a sermon. He *was* the sermon.'

James now mentors young professionals and reminds them: 'You don't need a pulpit to preach. Your life is a message. Make sure it's pointing to Jesus—because you might be the only Bible someone will ever read.'

EXPLORE MORE APHORISMS

- You can do what you please if what you do pleases God.

- You cannot start a fire in another's heart till it is burning in your own.

- You are rich when you are satisfied with what you have.

- You will never go hungry while the daily bread of grace is on the table of mercy.

- You are God's temple and His blueprint for your life; leave nothing to chance.

- You will never need more than He can supply, and what He supplies, both materially and spiritually, will always be enough.

- Your commitment to your family should be a lifetime; other relationships may have term limits.

- You are asking for trouble when you choose the wrong friends.

- You will become like the people you spend the most time with.

- You cannot be a leader if you don't learn to be a follower.

- You can't choose what happens to you, but you can choose how to respond.

- Your prayer should be, Loving God, help me make choices that will draw others to you.

- You can never tell what tomorrow brings, but what you do today will always affect your tomorrow.

- Your love for something today is at the expense of something tomorrow.

- You don't do everything you don't want to do and don't do everything you want to do.

- You cannot give what you don't have.

- You cannot be a champion until you think like a champion.

- Your point of contact determines your potential.

- You've got to move, you've got to move when the Lord is ready.

- You don't have to work for His grace; it is free.

- You should be right with God and wrong with man rather than right with man and wrong with God.

- You won the battle, not the war.

- You should not believe your feelings more than the Word which the Lord preaches to you.

- Your gifts should point people to Jesus.

- You are not alone until you are done.

- Your marriage vows are most important in those moments when they are most difficult to keep.

- You shall not die but live to declare the works of God in the land of the living.

- Your return on investment is one hundred per cent when you study the Bible each day.

- You will never get what you want if you wait for someone to bring it to you.

- Your God will get you through.

- You are not where you are "by accident" but rather by divine 'Royal' appointment.

- Your financial harvest is determined by what you spend, what you save and what you sow into God's Kingdom.

- Your father Abraham rejoiced to see my day, and he saw it and was glad (Jn. 8: 56). When did Abraham see Jesus? Check Genesis 22:13.

- You were not alone yesterday, you are not alone today and you are not going to be alone tomorrow, for Jesus is yesterday, today and forever (Emmanuel – God with us).

- Your prayer should be Jesus, give me the vision to see the weak places in my foundation that need attention.

- You don't talk about it; you will never give life to it.

- You give not because God needs something; you give because you need something.

- Your lifestyle will speak for you.

- Your secret of the Most High could be your bedroom, your morning commute on the bus, your desk in your office, a seat in the garden, a walk in the fresh air and anywhere can be that secret, special place with God.

- You are called to use your gifts to bless others.

- You don't have to study, practise or inherit the gifts of the spirit; remember it is a gift.

- You will never know what the future holds but God knows.

- Your physical and financial assets should include your spiritual assets too.

- You have not really learned the word until you live the word.

- You will never be at peace until you are at peace with God.

- You are not exempt from temptation, nor are you excluded from His provision.

- Your first goal is not to make your child happy; it is to teach him or her responsibility and happiness will follow.

- You have to fight through some bad days to earn the best days of your life.

- Your walk with Christ Jesus can produce fruit that blesses generations to come.

REFLECTION

The aphorisms highlight personal responsibility, spiritual identity, and the power of example in the Christian life. Each insight is an invitation to live intentionally, rooted in grace and committed to godly values. Let them stir you to live in alignment with God's purposes for your life and be a blessing to others.

APHORISM
Z

Zeal without wisdom can become a wildfire

Zion was a new believer—passionate, excited, and eager to tell the world about Jesus. Within weeks of his conversion, he was leading youth Bible studies, debating street preachers, and confronting church elders about doctrine.

He meant well, but his fiery passion often came with harsh words and little grace. He'd quote verses out of context, correct others publicly, and act without seeking counsel.

One Sunday, he preached in his small fellowship without permission. He spoke for over an hour with energy and boldness but left several confused and wounded.

The pastor gently pulled him aside after the service. 'Zion,' he said, 'your fire is real, but fire without boundaries can burn what God meant to build. Let your zeal be paired with wisdom.'

Those words humbled him. Zion began to submit to discipleship. He read not only Scripture but also sought understanding. He learned the power of listening before speaking, of grace before correction, and of prayer before action.

Years later, Zion became a beloved pastor—still passionate, but now deeply wise. When asked what changed him, he said:

'I learned that wildfire impresses crowds—but only refined fire transforms hearts. Zeal alone can burn bridges. But zeal with wisdom builds them.'

EXPLORE MORE APHORISMS

- Zion is not just a destination; it's a mindset of worship and hope.

- Zero tolerance for sin doesn't mean zero grace for the sinner.

- Zigzag journeys still lead to God's purposes.

- Zippers only work when both sides connect—so does fellowship.

- Zones of comfort rarely produce growth.

- Zebras don't change their stripes—but God changes hearts.

- Zeroing in on your calling sharpens your focus.

- Zest for life is found in serving others.

- Zones of prayer are zones of power.

REFLECTION

Zeal is a gift, but when untethered from wisdom, it can wound rather than heal. God desires passion that is refined by humility, guided by Scripture, and tempered with grace. True fire burns steadily—it warms, illuminates, and transforms. As you walk with Christ, let your enthusiasm be shaped by wisdom, so that your energy builds bridges, nurtures souls, and glorifies God rather than drawing attention to yourself.

Aphorisms to Explore – Stories for Further Reflection

THE BEAUTY
AND THE UGLY

In a quiet village wrapped in the whisper of ancient trees, two young girls lived: one renowned for her radiant beauty, the other marked by plainness that often drew cruel stares.

One day, a group of kidnappers seized the beautiful girl. Their mission was dark and resolute—they had been ordered to deliver a virgin to the Chief Fetish Priest, who would offer her life as a sacrifice to the gods.

But when the kidnappers unveiled the girl's face, they gasped. Her beauty was so striking that even hardened men of violence felt hesitation. Her wide, innocent eyes and delicate features stirred something human in them.

"She is too beautiful," one whispered. "To hand her over would be like spilling light into darkness," another muttered.

So, against their original orders, they released her. But fearing the wrath of their priest, they quickly searched for another. Soon, they found the plain girl—awkward, uncelebrated, often mocked for her looks. They seized her, reasoning, if the gods required a body, then this one would suffice.

When they brought her before the Fetish Priest, he scowled. "This girl?" he sneered. "She is unworthy of the gods. The offering must be flawless, pleasing to the spirits. Send her away!"

Thus, the first girl was spared because of her beauty, and the second girl was spared because of her lack of it.

Lesson: Beauty saved one, and ugliness saved another. So then—what are you complaining about? Too short? Too tall? Too thin, or too large? Too much nose, too little hair, a face that does not match the magazines? Perhaps what you despise in yourself is the very thing that protects you.

THE BABY CAMEL
AND ITS MUM

The desert stretched endlessly, a sea of golden sand under the blazing sun. In one corner of the zoo, however, the desert's noblest creature lived behind iron bars—a mother camel and her curious little calf.

One afternoon, as the air buzzed with the chatter of visitors, the baby camel tugged at its mother's side.

"Mum," it began, tilting its head, "Why do we have such big ears? They flap like palm leaves in the wind."

The mother camel smiled gently, lowering her head to nuzzle him, "Our ears are not just big, my son. They are shaped this way so that sand does not easily enter them when the desert storms rage. In the wilderness, this is our shield." The calf thought for a moment, then asked, "And why do we have these humps on our backs? They look so heavy!" The mother chuckled. "Those humps store water and fat. They allow us to walk for days—sometimes weeks—across dry lands without thirst or hunger slowing us down."

Still puzzled, the baby looked down at his own broad feet. "And what about these big, flat feet of ours? They look so clumsy compared to the gazelle's swift legs."

His mother answered with pride. "Our feet are wide and padded so they do not sink into the shifting sands. They are the secret to our endurance; the reason we can keep walking while other animals tire."

The calf's eyes widened in wonder. "So… we can endure storms, cross deserts without water, and walk without sinking into the sand? Then tell me, Mum… why are we here? Why are we locked in this zoo, while our gifts go unused?"

The mother fell silent. She turned her gaze to the horizon beyond the bars; her eyes clouded with sadness. "That, my child, is the real tragedy. We were made for the desert, not for cages. Our gifts are wasted here."

Lesson: Many Christians are like the camels—equipped by God with gifts to endure, overcome, and spread the Good News beyond the walls of the church. Yet many remain locked within, their abilities caged. What good are desert skills in a zoo?

THE THREE
FISH PRAYERS

In the quiet depths of a winding river, three little fish lived together. The waters shimmered in the sunlight above, but danger lurked everywhere—hungry sharks prowled, nets waited unseen, and shadows from above warned of predators in the sky.

One evening, the fish gathered under the shelter of some rocks. Their hearts were troubled, so they prayed aloud. To their amazement, the water around them glowed, and Jesus appeared, His presence filling the river with peace.

"My dear children," He said gently, "I have heard your prayers. Tell me, what would you like Me to do for you?"

The first fish darted forward eagerly.

"Lord, I want eyes all over my body! That way, I can see every danger from far away. No predator will ever surprise me."

Jesus looked at him with compassion. "Be it unto you." At once, the fish's body was covered in countless eyes, gleaming like tiny pearls. The fish swam proudly, able to see every ripple, every flicker of movement.

One day, he spotted a shark in the distance long before it arrived. Terrified, he sped away as fast as he could. But the shark was swifter, stronger, and soon overtook him. Despite all his eyes, the little fish was caught and devoured.

The second fish stepped forward next.

"Lord, give me wings! If danger comes, I will soar out of the river and escape to the sky."

"Be it unto you," Jesus said, and wings sprouted from the fish's sides, shimmering like silver. With joy, it tested them, flapping until it lifted out of the water, tasting the thrill of freedom.

Not long after, a shadow passed over the river. The winged fish spotted a predator approaching below and quickly leapt into the sky. But above, a hawk swooped down, talons sharp. The fish escaped the water, only to meet death in the air.

Finally, the third fish swam forward quietly. It bowed before Jesus and said, "Master, I do not want many eyes. I do not want wings. What I long for is Your presence. Give me Your protection, and I will be safe."

Jesus smiled, His voice warm like the sun through the water and said, "You have My protection."

And so that fish lived peacefully all its days in the river. While others trusted in their own cleverness and devices, this one trusted the hand of God. No net, no predator, no storm could touch it, for the Lord Himself was its shield.

Lesson: Many of us pray for clever strategies, more strength, or visible advantages to escape life's dangers. Yet the greatest protection is not in our inventions but in God's divine covering. What kind of protection are you praying for?

A Mother Scar Face and Her Daughter

❦

In a bustling town lived a mother and her only daughter. The mother's face bore deep scars—burns that etched across her cheeks and forehead like a story written in fire. To her, they were marks of sacrifice. To her daughter, they were a source of shame.

Whenever friends came over, the girl would whisper urgently, "Mum, please… go to your room. Don't let anyone see you." The mother, with a tender but heavy heart, obeyed. Time after time, she hid in the quiet of her bedroom while her daughter laughed with friends in the sitting room.

Years passed, and the girl grew into a fine young lady. One day, she came bouncing with excitement. "Mum! I'm throwing a birthday party here at home. All my classmates will come. You'll need to stay in your room again."

But this time, her mother did not move. Instead, she looked her daughter in the eye, her voice calm but firm.

"My child, do you know how I came by these scars you're so ashamed of?"

The daughter frowned and shrugged. "No. You've never told me."

Her mother drew in a slow breath, her mind returning to that night long ago. "When you were a baby," she began, "I was in the kitchen cooking while you slept peacefully in your cot. Suddenly, I smelled smoke. The fire spread quickly, and the bedroom where you lay was engulfed in flames. Without a thought for myself, I rushed in. The flames licked my face as I reached for you. I shielded you with my body, clutching you to my chest, and ran out through the smoke. You were safe—but my face was forever scarred."

Tears welled in the daughter's eyes. She had never imagined such a story lay behind the scars. Her heart broke as the weight of her shame crushed her spirit. She threw her arms around her mother's neck and sobbed, "Mum, I'm so sorry! I didn't know. Forgive me."

From that day onward, everything changed. She no longer hid her mother away. Instead, she proudly walked beside her at social events, introduced her to her friends, and spoke openly of the love that bore those scars.

Lesson: The daughter's shame is often our own. Many Christians hide the cross of Christ, embarrassed to speak of Him. Yet those scars—His wounds—were borne for our salvation. If we truly understood the price He paid, we would never be ashamed of Him.

The Crying
Devil

On a bright Sunday morning, a group of believers made their way joyfully to church. Their voices rose in laughter and song as they walked along the dusty road. The sun was warm, and the air seemed to hum with anticipation of worship.

But as they rounded a bend, they saw a strange sight—someone sitting on a rock by the roadside, shoulders slumped, face buried in his hands. His whole frame shook as though with sobs.

The group slowed. One of the brothers squinted and gasped. "Wait… isn't that—?"

"Yes," whispered another, "it's him. The Devil!"

The believers exchanged uneasy glances. Never had they seen Satan like this: not roaring, not threatening, but crying. Big, heavy tears ran down his face.

One bold brother stepped forward cautiously. "Why are you crying? Is it because you know we're going to pray fiercely today? Is it because we'll drive you back and torment you in the Spirit?"

The Devil lifted his head slowly, his eyes red and tired. His voice cracked as he spoke: "It is not your prayers that make me weep… but your lies."

The believers frowned in confusion.

The Devil continued, "You blame me for things I did not do. Every quarrel, every laziness, every poor choice—you stamp my name on it. 'The Devil made me do it,' you say, when it was your own weakness, your own stubbornness. You give me more credit than I deserve. I am weary of carrying the weight of your excuses."

Silence fell among the group. Their laughter was gone, replaced by uneasy reflection.

Finally, one sister whispered, "Have we really been lying against him... just to cover up our own shortcomings?"

The Devil stood, brushed off his cloak, and with one last sorrowful glance, disappeared into the shadows.

Lesson: It is easy to blame Satan for every mistake, failure, or sin. But often, the root lies in our own choices and lack of discipline. Instead of excusing ourselves, we must face the truth: not all battles are from the Devil—some are from within.

THE CROSS
OF A WOMAN

One night, a weary woman drifted into a troubled sleep. In her dream, she stood in a vast hall filled with wooden crosses of every shape and size. Some were towering and heavy, others small and crooked, but all were marked with names.

The woman clutched her own cross tightly against her chest, groaning. "Lord," she cried, "this burden is too heavy for me. Why must my life be so hard? Others seem to have it easier. I cannot carry this any longer."

Suddenly, Jesus appeared beside her, His face gentle but His eyes searching. "Daughter," He said softly, "if you believe your cross is heavier than others, then let us see. Write your name upon it."

She bent down and carved her name into the wood. Then, with a wave of His hand, Jesus turned all the crosses upside down so the names were hidden beneath them.

"Now," He instructed, "choose any cross you wish. Lift it, and if it is lighter, it will be yours."

Hope filled her heart. She walked among the endless rows, her eyes scanning the crosses. She tried lifting one—its weight nearly crushed her. She tried another—still unbearable. One by one, she tested them, each heavier than the last.

At last, exhausted and trembling, she bent down to a smaller cross in the corner. To her surprise, it was lighter, more bearable. She clutched it to her chest with relief.

Jesus smiled gently. "Turn it over, my child. See who's cross you now carry."

She turned it, and her breath caught in her throat. There, carved into the wood, was her own name. It was the very cross she had laid down at the beginning.

Tears filled her eyes. "So... mine was never the heaviest after all."

Jesus placed a hand on her shoulder. "I do not give you a burden you cannot bear. Your cross is fitted for you, just as others have their own. Learn to trust My wisdom and carry it with patience. For with every cross comes My grace."

Lesson: God will never give us more than we can endure. Often, we envy others or complain about our struggles, not realising that their burdens may be heavier than ours. Be content, and trust that your cross has been measured perfectly by a loving Father.

THE PRESIDING ELDER AND THE GOURD

In a small village assembly stood a man whose devotion to God was admired by all—the Presiding Elder. Though he lived in poverty, his zeal for the Lord was unmatched. He was always the first to arrive at church, often sweeping the dusty floor and arranging the benches long before the members gathered. Sometimes he would kneel in prayer for half an hour, interceding for the congregation with tears.

His faithfulness made him a pillar of the fellowship, though at home his life was hard. His farm yielded little, his pockets were empty, and he often wondered how he would provide for his family. Yet, he never stopped serving.

One day, while weeding his farm under the hot sun, his cutlass slipped and struck one of the gourds he had planted near the boundary. To his shock, instead of seeds or pulp, the gourd cracked open to reveal glittering nuggets of gold.

The elder dropped to his knees, trembling. "Oh, Lord! You have answered my prayers! No more poverty, no more lack. My suffering is over."

From that day on, everything changed. Afraid someone might discover his treasure, he began guarding the gourds carefully. Instead of being the first at church, he arrived late—or not at all. His excuses grew thin, but his fear of losing the gourds grew stronger.

The presbyters noticed the shift. Concerned, they approached him gently. "Elder, what troubles you? Why have you forsaken the zeal you once had?"

Ashamed but unable to keep his secret, he confessed. "Brothers, the Lord has blessed me! These gourds are filled with gold. I must protect them, lest I return to poverty. Forgive my absence, but I cannot neglect this gift."

The presbyters exchanged uneasy glances. One of them stepped forward. "Elder, are you sure? God blesses, yes, but He does not distract us from His work. I do not believe those gourds contain gold."

The elder, stung by disbelief, grew defensive. "You doubt me? Then I will prove it!" He rushed to the farm, followed by the brethren, and seized a gourd. With a swift stroke, he split it open. To his horror, it was empty—just pulp and seeds.

"No… no… perhaps another!" He hacked open a second, then a third, then a fourth. But each one was the same. There was no gold, only the fruit of the earth.

The elder's knees buckled. His eyes filled with despair. He realised that in his greed, he had abandoned his calling, forsaken his first love, and traded his peace for an illusion.

The presbyters placed their hands on his shoulder. One whispered, "Brother, remember the Word: The love of money is the root of all evil, which while some have coveted after, they have pierced themselves with many sorrows."

The elder bowed his head and wept.

Lesson: Contentment is the true treasure. Chasing wealth at the expense of faith can blind us, deceive us, and leave us empty. Riches without God vanish, but service to Him endures forever.

THE RICH MAN
AND THE PAINTER

Every morning, a poor painter climbed his rickety scaffolding, his hands stained with colour, his face beaming with joy. As he brushed walls with strokes of blue and gold, his voice rose in song. Passersby often paused, marvelling not at the paint but at the painter's happiness.

One of those passersby was a wealthy man who owned many lands and houses. Day after day, he saw the painter high above the ground, whistling, singing hymns, and laughing as though the world itself was a canvas he delighted in.

Finally, curiosity overcame him. One afternoon, as the painter descended from his scaffold, the rich man stopped him. "Tell me," The rich man said, adjusting his fine cloak, "why are you always so happy? You hang dangerously from that height. One slip and you could die. Yet you sing as though you have everything."

The painter smiled, wiping his hands on his worn trousers. "Sir, I have my work, I have my daily bread, and I have peace in my heart. What more could I ask for?"

The rich man frowned. "Peace? With so little? Nonsense. Here—take this." He thrust a heavy purse of coins into the painter's hand. "It is a fortune. Stop this risky job. Enjoy life."

The painter hesitated but finally accepted, overwhelmed by the sheer weight of the money. For the first time in his life, he was rich.

But that night, he could not sleep. He turned restlessly on his bed, his mind racing. What if thieves come for the money? Where should I hide it? How should I spend it? What if I lose it all?

Day after day, the worry grew. The purse of gold became a chain around his neck. The songs that once poured freely from his lips were gone. His brushes lay unused, his scaffold empty. The peace he once carried had evaporated, replaced by sleepless nights and gnawing fear.

At last, unable to bear it, the painter returned to the rich man. His eyes were weary, his voice heavy. "Sir, take back your money. Since I accepted it, my joy has fled, my peace is gone, and my heart is restless. Better to be poor and happy than rich and tormented."

The rich man was silent, struck by the irony. He had wealth but no peace, and he had stolen peace from one who had nothing but contentment.

The painter climbed back onto his scaffold, picked up his brush, and began to sing once more.

Lesson: Joy is not bought with wealth, nor is peace stored in a purse of gold. One can be poor yet content, or rich yet empty. True happiness lies not in riches, but in a heart at rest.

THE RICE FARMER AND HIS PET PARROT

❧

In a quiet village surrounded by endless green fields, there lived a humble rice farmer. His days began before sunrise, his feet sinking into the muddy water as he tended his crops with patient care. Though life was hard, he had a companion that lightened his heart—his pet parrot.

This was no ordinary parrot. It was intelligent, quick to learn, and loyal. The farmer loved it dearly, often bringing it along when he worked in the fields. As he weeded the rice beds, the parrot perched nearby, chattering cheerfully, sometimes even mimicking the farmer's words.

But there was one problem: the rice fields often attracted swarms of birds that came to feed greedily on his crops. The farmer, desperate to protect his livelihood, would take up his gun and fire into the air to scare them away. Many times, he hit one or two birds, sending the rest scattering in fear.

One evening, as the sun melted into the horizon, he noticed a huge flock of birds descending on his rice field. Frustrated, he raised his gun, aimed, and fired. A bird fell to the ground, flapping helplessly.

The farmer walked over, expecting to find a wild bird. But when he looked closer, his heart sank—it was his own beloved parrot, wounded and gasping.

The farmer dropped to his knees, tears filling his eyes. "Oh no… my friend, my companion… I didn't mean for this to happen!" The parrot opened its beak weakly and whispered its final words: "Bad company…bad company." And with that, the parrot fell still.

The farmer buried his pet with trembling hands, his heart heavy with regret. From that day on, the echo of those final words haunted him.

Lesson: The Bible warns, "Do not be misled: Bad company corrupts good character." (1 Corinthians 15:33). The parrot, once wise and innocent, fell because it was among those who brought destruction. So too in life, our companions shape our destiny. Who we walk with matters.